MAMMALS

MICHAEL CLARK

D1343798

CHANCELLOR
PRESS

HOW TO USE THIS BOOK

SEROTINE
.Lf 5cm. A serotine bat with a
juvenile on her fur. She is a
large, dark-faced species.

This guide covers over 100 species of
European mammal, many of which can be
observed in the UK. The identification
pages (42-125) give the common English
name, the length in centimetres, and
some useful information, on habits or
habitat, for example. The lengths (L) - or
standard forearm lengths (Lf) for bats -
are given as a range in most cases, but
there is always great variety between
young and old and from area to area
throughout Europe. Each species section
includes a box called 'Tracker Points'.
These are a variety of signs to look for when
tracking a mammal, including footprints,
droppings and food remains, which indicate
the type of mammals in the area.

ACKNOWLEDGEMENTS

The author and publishers would like to thank the
following individuals for their assistance in the
preparation of this book · Andrew Branson of
British Wildlife Publishing, Principal Consultant ·
Sarah Castell, Designer · David Christie, Editorial
Consultant · Dr Gordon Corbet, for inspiration ·
Derek Hall, who conceived the series · and
Cathy Percival, for processing the text.

First published by Hamlyn,
a division of Octopus Publishing Group Ltd

This edition published in 2000
by Chancellor Press, an imprint of Bounty Books,
a division of Octopus Publishing Group Ltd,
2-4 Heron Quays, London E14 4JP

Printed in Italy

CONTENTS

INTRODUCTION

GENERAL CHARACTERISTICS

A badger with her litter; usually two to three cubs.

Mammals have adapted to life in woodland, rivers, estuaries, seas, land, the air, mountains and desert. Of about 4,000 world species, about 200 live in and around Europe. The female of any mammal species has the vital role of rearing the next generation. A typical feature is her milk or mammary (hence the name 'mammal') glands with which to feed her young. Most mammals have hair on their bodies which moults to be thin in the summer, but is thick in the winter. They also have a big brain inside their alert head, which enables them to learn quickly from experience, and retain memory so that they can undertake quite complicated behaviour such as finding food and a safe home. They have a strong internal skeleton of bones, including toes on four limbs, plus a tail which, like the ears, can be very obvious. They can control their body heat over a wide range of weather conditions.

A common dolphin, one of the many types of toothed whales adapted to life in the sea. Flippers replace fore-limbs; tail flukes and back fins give movement with stability; the young suckle milk from mammaries.

Common shrew ▲
The faces of mammals come in all shapes and sizes: insect-eaters have long noses, sharp teeth and sensitive whiskers.

Long-eared bat ▶
Bats eat insects and have sharp teeth but, because they fly by echolocation (measuring the position of an object using echo), the ears are complex.

◀ **Common seal**
Marine species are streamlined without obvious ears, and have long whiskers and large mouths to detect and catch fish.

PILOT WHALE ▽
Whales breathe through air holes on the top of their heads; and some have advanced sonar systems to navigate by.

CHAMOIS ▶
Herbivorous species have long jaws for chewing and may also sport strong horns (or antlers, in deer) on their heads.

PROJECT

Mammal skulls are very beautiful structures and give an insight into how each species is classified. Bury your specimen and mark the site with a labelled stick. When just the bones are left, ask your parents to help you clean them by soaking in diluted domestic bleach or hydrogen peroxide (Warning: do not attempt this unsupervised). Always wear gloves and take care!

LIFESTYLES

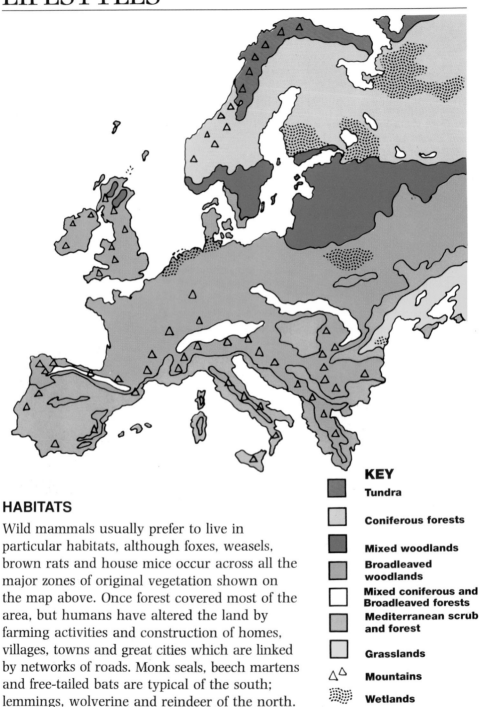

HABITATS

Wild mammals usually prefer to live in particular habitats, although foxes, weasels, brown rats and house mice occur across all the major zones of original vegetation shown on the map above. Once forest covered most of the area, but humans have altered the land by farming activities and construction of homes, villages, towns and great cities which are linked by networks of roads. Monk seals, beech martens and free-tailed bats are typical of the south; lemmings, wolverine and reindeer of the north.

KEY

- Tundra
- Coniferous forests
- Mixed woodlands
- Broadleaved woodlands
- Mixed coniferous and Broadleaved forests
- Mediterranean scrub and forest
- Grasslands
- △△ Mountains
- Wetlands

Domestication

Mammals have been tamed by humans for thousands of years. Wolves were bred into many types of dogs for herding livestock, guarding and hunting. Sheep, goats and cows were valuable for providing food, clothing and milk. Horses were the major power for transport and ploughing, well into this century. Pigs, descended from native wild boar, are a useful source of food.

Wildlife sites

You get much more out of visits to national parks, nature reserves and conservation centres if you plan ahead: buy a map, and find out if boat trips, for example, can be booked. Libraries have reference books and maps, as well as information on local natural history societies and wildlife trusts. Tourist boards can help you, too.

PROJECT

Plaster casts are fun to make, and will leave you with souvenirs of your mammal-watching. Clip some cardboard into a circle or square, and place it over a track in the mud. Mix plaster of Paris with clean streamwater, and pour into the mould. Leave to set (about 15 mins) then dig it up.

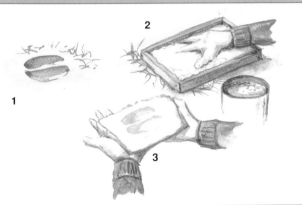

EQUIPMENT

IN THE FIELD

Wear clothing which will keep you warm and comfortable. It must not be noisy as you walk, and it should help you merge into your surroundings. Rainproof oiled jackets with matching hats and dark-coloured mittens are popular. Black or blue as well as light trousers show up badly: stick to dark greens or dull browns. Wellingtons or walking boots will keep your feet dry in most situations. Binoculars are the most flexible aid to watching and, because mammals are usually active in poor light conditions, stick to ones marked 10 x 40 or thereabouts. Telescopes are becoming popular, and are particularly good on a tripod in coastal or mountain areas. Most dealers allow you to try out different makes to see which suits.

Testing your binoculars before you buy them is very important. Always check for alignment and ensure that they do not 'bend' or distort the image you are focusing on, and that you are seeing only one image of the mammal in the lens!

Take binoculars with you at all times when in the countryside or on trips, even when you do not expect to use them. If buying a pair, try out as many as possible. Ask yourself: do they feel too heavy, too small; do they give a clear, sharp picture? Small, light binoculars are best, since the larger types can strain the neck or shoulders. Make sure the strap is strong.

◁ Take notes on the spot with date and locality. Get used to maps and using grid references to pin-point records. A light compass as used in orienteering and hill walking is helpful, especially in new country where you might get lost.

Light seats make watching ▷ more comfortable. A relaxed tracker is a better observer. Take plastic bags for specimens or to sit on.

◁ A useful selection of equipment to have with you would include tubs and dishes for anything you may want to save, a trowel and tweezers to dig in the soil, and a bean bag (or an inflatable cushion) to sit on.

PHOTOGRAPHY

Photographs record a moment of time, and can be a very valuable reference to things you have seen. If you keep a diary, it is useful to have colour prints to stick in from your time spent watching, but local societies are good fun to join and members have slide shows to share their experiences. If you want to enter competitions, make sure your pictures are sharp and well composed. You do not have to take pictures of rare things to get top results. The single-lens reflex camera with flash is the most popular type used.

Wild mammals get used to hides and will come readily to take food as long as it is regularly provided for them. Set up your camera beforehand to avoid any disturbance to the animal. Do not let photography distract you from watching.

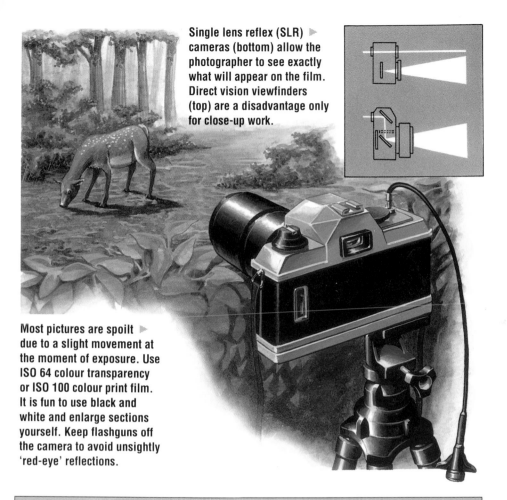

Single lens reflex (SLR) ▷ cameras (bottom) allow the photographer to see exactly what will appear on the film. Direct vision viewfinders (top) are a disadvantage only for close-up work.

Most pictures are spoilt ▷ due to a slight movement at the moment of exposure. Use ISO 64 colour transparency or ISO 100 colour print film. It is fun to use black and white and enlarge sections yourself. Keep flashguns off the camera to avoid unsightly 'red-eye' reflections.

PROJECT

Famous professional photographers like David Hosking make portable sets for small mammals, which are almost impossible to photograph well in the wild. Openings in the sides allow several flashguns to be used at different angles, connected to the camera to give the best lighting possible. You can make these with natural vegetation arranged inside. High-speed electronic flash is able to 'freeze' any movement of very active animals, and pictures must be pin-sharp for reproduction in books and magazines.

FIELDCRAFT

You must learn to move quietly and not make sudden movements, whenever and wherever you watch wild mammals. It is the human shape and scent which cause most fear, and this is why people on horses or hidden inside vehicles do not cause deer, boar, wild sheep or goats much fear unless they dismount or stand clear to show their true identity. Fieldcraft comes with experience, but some important rules for the silent, slow tracker are shown on these pages.

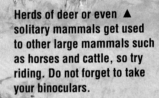

Herds of deer or even ▲ solitary mammals get used to other large mammals such as horses and cattle, so try riding. Do not forget to take your binoculars.

If you suddenly show up ▲ above a skyline, do not be surprised if everything runs away. Remember, however, that bears have been known to charge.

Crumbled-up dry leaves ►
can be used to check the
wind direction.

Deer like to browse on ▲
brambles which grow in
clearings. Watch from a
distance.

When you are watching ►
mammals in the countryside,
it is important not to make a
loud noise by cracking twigs
underfoot, speaking loudly
or even shouting.

MAKING FIELD NOTES

It is very important to take accurate notes when observing mammals. The great naturalists of the past were able to write about what they saw because they took accurate notes at the time. It is now very easy to buy waterproof notebooks which do not go soggy in your pocket after heavy rain. Useful points to note are: name (if known), length, colour, location, when it was seen, tracks, droppings and any unusual features. A note on the spot is worth endless attempts to recall details!

Drawings are helpful for later reference and you can seek out field signs where you see a mammal or find one dead. Footprints, droppings and the location tell you much. Field voles, for example, prefer grassland and shun shade from trees or shrubs. Always relate mammals to their habitats and homes.

If you find drawing is difficult, get used to drawing the simple silhouettes of a number of typical mammal types. Red deer (top left) are rectangular with four long legs plus antlers. The fox (bottom left) has a bushy tail, pointed face and ears. Badgers (bottom) are low to the ground with short legs. Squirrels and mice (top right) feature distinct ear and tail shapes.

Field signs include vole, weasel, rabbit and deer droppings and a badger latrine excavated by a tree with a gnawed bark. Tracks lead to a little tree pool.

To identify tracks of the species shown in the silhouettes, measure and draw (better, photograph) to record the right owners.

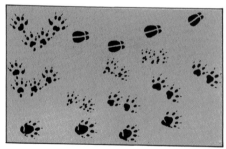

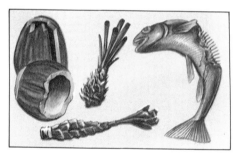

When bat watching it is important for accurate records to note the times you first see them, how long they fly for and how closely they follow dusk (or dawn) around the year. At roosts you can clock the first flights of young bats, too.

Feeding signs need careful analysis to identify which of several species may be involved. Keep nuts and cones to see how they were opened: by voles, mice or squirrels? You will not want to keep half-eaten fish: from otter or mink?

CONCEALMENT

The ground always seems hard, so carry a light hammer with you to knock poles in firmly.

Tie the poles together ▷ with strong cord to give the basic frame strength at each corner.

◁ It is important for a hide to withstand strong winds, so lash up the structure firmly.

Movement frightens ▷ wildlife: ensure your hide is stable, and cut a hole for clear viewing.

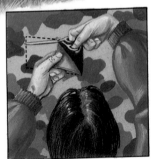

HIDES

A hide can be almost any structure which disguises your shape. If you know animals are watching your approach, a good technique is to take a friend into the hide with you and then leave, allowing the animal to assume that you, too, have left. Mostly hides are used in places where you expect mammals to emerge from their retreats, homes or courtship sites. Vandalism is always a risk, so it is better to erect the structure only for a limited time.

Camouflage-coloured ▲ canvas, a drab string net with natural foliage pushed amongst the sides and dark green tarpaulin are all effective materials and, although ready-made products are available, it is better fun and cheaper to make up your own design for particular needs. Use guy ropes if necessary.

If you can get permission in a little-visited locality to build a safe structure, tree platforms are excellent because scent drifts upwards. On the ground, even when downwind, wild mammals may catch the smell of humans and run off. Ensure that the hide is not too high from the ground, and never use nails in its construction.

Do not feel that you must make an elaborate structure to see or photograph mammals: a simple screen of canvas or pigeon-hide leaf netting can be quickly tied up at a place where you have come across active water voles, for example. Weasels and stoats frequently re-emerge after seeing you, and so a quickly put-up 'blind' may be sufficient to conceal you from them.

HOW TO WATCH

The most effective long-term hides are permanent structures built like garden sheds, with which wildlife become familiar. These are to be found at nature reserves, etc. They can be baited each evening and illuminated on a time switch that animals get used to. A pipe in the roof can give ventilation, and access for people with mobility problems should always be constructed. Arthur Bate from Stevenage College helped design this hide.

PLANNING A TRIP

CAREFUL PREPARATION

You should take binoculars and notebook, and spare pens or pencils, whenever you go out watching wildlife. At new sites or in remote countryside, a compass and preparatory research into weather forecasts, tide timetables and large-scale maps are important, too. Mammal watching often sees you at times when most people are at home: dusk, night-time and dawn. It is vital that you should leave a route plan of where you are going, and estimate times at grid references on the map. In hilly or mountainous areas it is better to go with a companion.

Information
On expeditions learn to read maps properly, or go with someone who does, and keep asking them about contour lines, grid references and compass bearings until you know the techniques yourself. Check all the relevant local information such as tide times if you plan to watch otters or seals in an estuary. Tidal water can race across mudflats faster than you can run!

If you go out to watch bats at night it is safer to go with a friend. Remember that visits to roosts must be organised by a licensed bat worker in your local Bat Group. This is a common long-eared bat.It is usually found in woods and house roofs. Watching at a hide with a lamp set to come on each night, you will be able to see bats chasing moths attracted by the illumination.

Dogs can be fun on walks, but make sure you keep them under control. They must never roam the countryside or worry live-stock. Unfortunately, dogs tend to disperse wildlife ahead of you unless they are very well trained. Close all gates behind you. Some dogs have been specially trained to herd sheep, usually border collies. These are the only dogs which should be allowed near sheep. Farmers insist a dog is kept on a lead even if you are a few fields away.

CODE OF CONDUCT

You must treat all wildlife and the countryside with care and respect. In June you may come across a fawn born in long grass, because the mother was feeding there. Fawns born in deep undergrowth in the daytime are usually out of sight. They are not abandoned, and you must not handle the fawn. A quick photograph is alright, but the mother may desert the fawn if she finds that it smells of your scent.

DECIDUOUS WOODLAND

Deciduous trees shed all their leaves annually at the end of the growing season. They support a far greater range of insects and plants on and underneath their canopy than fir trees. They also create a more diverse leaf litter for mammals to live in and find food. The woodland provides cover for badgers, foxes and deer which feed out in the surrounding open areas. A wood need not be large for there to be a great deal of mammal activity, either in the day or at night.

Bat ▼
It is often less common bat species which frequent woodland.

Fallow deer ▼
Fallow deer come in many shades from black to spotted, and sometimes pure white.

It is best to walk slowly ▲ along a woodland edge at twilight, stop every few steps and check any movement with a camera or your binoculars.

Fox ▶
Foxes are usually the first large mammal abroad in late afternoon, or as darkness begins to gather.

Wood mouse ▶
Wood mice are strictly night animals, and can scuttle along the woodland floor with amazing speed.

A prominent tree stump can be baited with food such as peanut butter to attract a variety of mammals, such as martens, squirrels, foxes, badgers. It must be baited and observed regularly to be a success.

Wild boar ▼
Wild boar stay in small groups or move out from cover alone to feed.

Badger ▼
Badgers live in colonies, and scent the air cautiously before emerging from their underground setts.

Dormouse ▲
There are several types of dormouse in Europe, but all are rather exclusive and local to old woodlands or big gardens.

Hedgehog ▶
Hedgehogs love a damp night on which to emerge from their nests.

CONIFEROUS WOODLAND

Coniferous trees typically have evergreen foliage, shed at the end of a period of growth, and bear cones. They tend to shade the forest floor, and have less diversity of life than deciduous woodland. Conifers provide shelter and limited food for many mammals, but the numbers of species become fewer, and more specialised to a cold climate, the further north you venture. These are the last trees in mountain areas before the exposure becomes too great to support growth.

Wolverine ▼
A wolverine has scented carrion. Pale markings show it is not a bear, very few of which remain.

◄ Arctic fox
Arctic foxes may travel hundreds of kilometres in winter to feed by the sea, or in milder conditions.

Birch mouse ▲
Where the birch trees give way to evergreen conifers, birch mice live. They hibernate in winter.

In summer, look for ▶
polecat breeding earths near
the borders of conifer
plantations, where kittens
may play at dusk. The scent
is distinctive.

Reindeer ▼
Reindeer feed out onto the
tundra from woodland. They
dig at snow to get to the
hidden plants in winter.

Elk ▼
Moose eat aquatic plants,
and abandon wading only
when the ice freezes lakes
and ponds.

Polecat ▼
Polecats like to live in
forests in river valleys,
where there is ample food
and water.

MEDITERRANEAN SCRUB

Conditions get very hot indeed in July and August: by far the best times for the tracker to visit Mediterranean countries are in spring and autumn. The flora has 'burnt out' by the end of May, and wild sheep and goats such as mouflon and ibex will move higher into the mountains. Take ample supplies of soft drink with you, and keep to dawn and dusk, rather than mid-day, sorties.

Rock mouse ▼
Rock mice are one of the many interesting varieties of small mammal in the dry scrub. Active after dusk.

Donkey and goat ▲
Donkeys and goats are vital means of transport for food-stuffs and goods in small village communities.

Beech marten ▲
Beech martens are very shy and nocturnal, but you may even see one teasing a passing tortoise.

Bat ▼
The warm, dry climate, with
ample insects, results in an
abundance of many species
of bat.

Bat ▼
At dusk, typical bats include
pipistrelle, whiskered and
horseshoe, often streaming
from big roosts in buildings.

The pine marten eats a variety of food: ▲
from squirrels, small birds and voles, to
fruit and honey.

FRESH WATER

Water is a focus for wild mammals, and some species are particularly adapted to live in and around streams, rivers, canals and lakes. Because of the lush vegetation associated with the water margins, protection, food and nesting materials are readily available. The more trees are allowed to grow on banks, and their roots to spread into the water, the better.

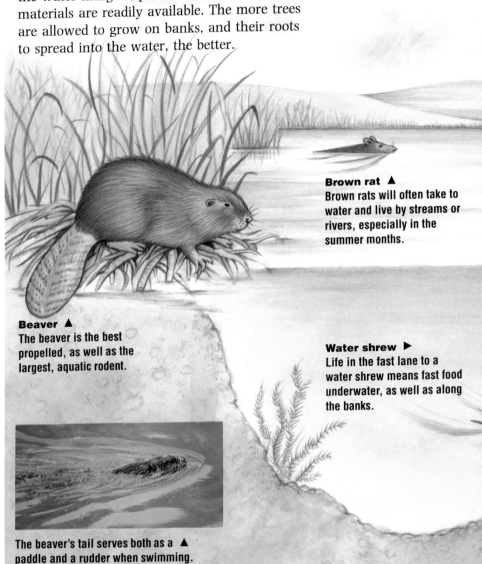

Brown rat ▲
Brown rats will often take to water and live by streams or rivers, especially in the summer months.

Beaver ▲
The beaver is the best propelled, as well as the largest, aquatic rodent.

Water shrew ▶
Life in the fast lane to a water shrew means fast food underwater, as well as along the banks.

The beaver's tail serves both as a ▲ paddle and a rudder when swimming.

Bat ▼
Daubenton's bats feed later than most, just after dusk, as the caddisflies and other insects hatch on the water's surface.

Harvest mouse ▼
Harvest mice climb amongst the dense marsh grasses and plants where their nests are easily constructed.

Water vole ▲
Water voles enjoy picnics by the water's edge and, if annoyed by wasps or ants, can slip into the water at a moment's notice.

You can help in national and local ▲ surveys of rivers to see if otters are recovering their numbers yet. Rocks under bridges are good viewing sites. The picture shows an otter slide.

THE COASTLINE

The more remote and undisturbed a coastline, the more you are likely to see wild mammals, as well as seabirds and wild flowers. Tidelines always attract animals who have discovered that food is concentrated there. Red deer eat seaweed, for example, and, at the opposite end of the scale, shrews know that insects breed in the stones worn away from rocks. Out in the sea, seals and dolphins may be in the vicinity.

Fox ▼
Foxes learn to scavenge along beaches after visitors have gone, and live in cliff scrub habitats throughout Europe.

Dolphin ▲
Bottle-nosed dolphins like company, and sometimes one may stay around a shore and play with bathers.

Seal ▶
Grey seal breeding colonies are usually noisy places because they call and squabble between themselves in the autumn.

PROJECT

Take a bag or basket, and search amongst the tide line and rocks for items washed up with the seaweed. Seal skulls and other bones may turn up, especially after a gale. They will need a good clean when you get home. Also collect any dangerous litter such as broken glass, which can harm humans and animals alike. If you take care of the environment of mammals, fewer will be hurt due to negligence. Get in the habit of always carrying a plastic bag or two in your pocket when mammal watching.

Killer whale ▼
Killer whales have an air of menace about them as they come inshore.

Seal ▲
Seals often bob head-up off-shore in the water. They look around, floating upright, with flippers to steady them.

Otter ▲
Otters live well on seafoods, especially around the northern islands and inlets. Tides bring in fresh food as the turbulence of the water stirs up marine life.

LOWLAND PASTURE

Where hedgerows have been left or are being re-planted, a rich variety of mammals can find plenty to feed on in late summer. All the fruiting species of trees and shrubs have flowers, and are now covered in berries, nuts, mast and larger fruit. Permanent pasture produces the best flora and insect life, especially if it is properly managed, so that there is food for small mammals, and they in turn provide food for the larger species.

Grey squirrel ▼
You can hear pieces of shell rain down from the tree canopy as squirrels gorge themselves on nuts.

Rabbit ▼
The last of the summer rabbit litters are playing within a safe distance of protective cover.

◄ Bank vole
Bank voles will enjoy rose hip seeds, and climb for nuts if they are being plundered above them.

Mole ▼
Young moles are forced to leave the favoured woodland burrows of their parents and dig new homes in the open.

Squirrel drey ▶
Beech trees give valuable mast seeds for birds and mammals. A summer squirrel drey is on a limb.

The hare has colonized ▲ all sorts of environments, but is most common in the lowlands.

Roe deer ▼
Roe are very mobile in July–August, and bucks can display rutting behaviour again in the early autumn.

Polecat ▼
Polecats are recovering their numbers in places. They run at rabbits with great speed to catch them.

Stoat ▼
Stoats may lose a rabbit they catch because it screams and attracts foxes or people. They do not challenge polecats for theirs.

LOWLAND ARABLE

Demands to increase farm production this century have seen very dramatic changes to arable areas, so that many Victorian farmers would not recognise the land where they worked if they returned today. As well as sweeping hedgerow, woodland and dell removals, drainage has taken away much botanical, and thus animal, life, and crops may be saturated with as many as six treatments of fertilizers, herbicides, fungicides and insecticides each growing season.

Chinese water deer ▼
Water deer like to lie up in ditches and graze, since the lowland arable surroundings are similar to the marshy habitats of home in China.

Hare ▼
Hares have declined this century, but may recover well as farming becomes more organic and varied.

Field vole ▼
Voles breed on the edges of paths and fields, and enjoy the crops, as well as the wild grasses, seeds and fruits.

Yellow-necked mouse ▼
Yellow-necked mice are very
energetic climbers, and will
explore for food from the
ground cover up into trees.

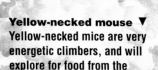

PROJECT

Harvest time varies according to the
weather and type of crop, but usually
peaks around August. It is exciting to
watch a combine-harvester at work and
see if hares, rabbits, foxes or deer may
be disturbed out of cover right in front of
you. There may be other mammal
species – and birds – present to record.

Common hamster ▼
Although common hamsters
are typical of open rough
grassland, they can also be
found on cultivated field
edges in C and E Europe.

Shrew ▼
You only see several shrews
together when a family is
growing up. Otherwise, they
keep to themselves near
hedges and countryside paths.

HILLY LOWLAND

In Europe many areas are famous for the way hillsides are farmed to produce varieties of wines. They are examples of intensive management which includes skilful pruning and collection of the produce, as well as the ancient arts of fermentation and preservation. Chemicals are used and much is mechanised, but rural hilly lowlands have an abundance of small mammals and their predators.

◀ **Bee orchid**
The beautiful flowers of orchids are often nibbled by mice or voles, which enjoy the honey-like nectar.

Weasel ▼
Weasels run along paths and surprise mice or voles which, owing to their size, they can also follow into their nests.

Common vole ▼
Common voles like to tunnel more than field voles, and thus survive better when a pasture is closely grazed.

Long-eared bat ▶
Long-eared bats are useful predators of insects on vines, and can pick them off the leaves or stems in flight.

Garden dormouse ▶
Garden dormice often make distinctive calls, and enjoy the fruits of the herbaceous borders or orchard.

Stoat ▲
Stoats are creatures of habit: and if you see one hunting it is worth watching again at the same place and time.

Some vineyards will give you a tour ▲ of the buildings. It is worth asking if the people who work there have noticed bat roosts, have mice around the work areas or know of a particular species of mammal in the vineyard. They may direct you to someone who works in the hills and knows more.

URBAN MAMMALS

Humans have failed to keep their population at a sensible size, and have built over so much land that wildlife has increasingly had to adapt to the miniature versions of the countryside we call gardens. In these, people can have complete control over the trees, shrubs, flowers and vegetables they grow. All kinds of species are muddled together from all over the world, and local plants and animals may be discouraged.

Bat ▲
Pipistrelle bats roost in cavity walls, and noctule bats feed over park lakes.

PROJECT

Bat boxes are easy to construct and are roughly the same size as bird boxes, but without a hole in the front. Make using thick, rough wood, about 10cm square inside. Secure firmly to a wall or tree and, after three or four years, it may attract roosting bats. Contact the Mammal Society for details of workshops you may like to join.

Squirrel ▶
There may be several squirrels present, even if you think it is just one stealing bird food.

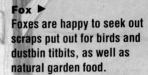

Fox ▶
Foxes are happy to seek out scraps put out for birds and dustbin titbits, as well as natural garden food.

Tawny owl ▲
Tawny owls help reduce the
rat population, which can
exploit food put out for
other species.

Rat ▼
Rats are scavengers, eating
any scraps of food they are
able to find.

An urban lawn is a perfect feeding area for ▲
night visitors because you can illuminate it
from the house. Hedgehogs are often
frequent night visitors.

Hedgehog ▲
Hedgehogs make tours of
gardens and parks to feed on
worms, insects and food put
out for them on plates.

MOUNTAINOUS WOODLAND

Although you must respect the weather conditions and steep terrain, some of the most interesting wild mammals in Europe live in the mountain regions (e.g. the Pyrenees). The country code applies everywhere, but in the mountains an additional danger is throwing or rolling rocks down fields: avalanches may be a direct result. Never run down-hill, because the human body cannot stop without falling in such circumstances.

Lynx ◄
The silent, nocturnal lynx is a rare predatory cat, which keeps hunting all through the winter.

Chamois ▼
Chamois are more often found in the shelter of forests in winter, when their coats change to dark brown.

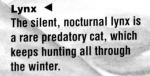

Wild cat ►
Wild cats have no trouble in climbing over rocks and boulders, where their dens are usually located.

Until heavy snow falls you can seek out ▲ the burrow systems of the Alpine marmots. See if gathered hay has been left outside.

Pine marten ▶
Pine martens will chase squirrels, although smaller mammals and fruits are more typical food.

Marmot ▼
Small mammals may feed, and even breed, under the insulation of snow. Marmots hibernate in a cosy nest underground.

◀ **Red squirrel**
Pines are favoured by red squirrels for their cones. The squirrels build dreys in the branches.

THROUGH THE SEASONS

There is always something happening in the world of mammals, even if some species are keeping a low profile in the winter months. To enjoy seeing the protected species as well as general mammals, join your local Natural History Society, Wildlife Trust and the Mammal Society. In these societies you will meet the other people who are enthusiastic about the natural world. Bat roosts, for example, can be visited only with a licensed person, and you may want to progress to this sort of position of trust yourself.

Winter ▽

Although bats and hedgehogs hibernate in the cold months, they can be active in mild weather. Dormice tuck well away from view in cosy nests; shrews have to keep rushing around to find active insects however cold it is; and spare a thought for the common seal in a winter gale being buffeted about in a cold sea.

Spring ▷

In spring, you have much to look forward to as the squirrels start to have litters in dreys up in the tree tops. Badgers and foxes soon have cubs; red, and other large species of deer, lose their antlers. The lengthening daylight hours will really tempt you out after the darkness of the winter.

Summer ▲

By summer, the pups are being born to common seals on our shores; fawns are born in lush vegetation and will soon be walking with their mothers. Litters of rabbits become a common sight and leap with playful kicks of their back feet as they dive for cover; and bats are soon breeding in their favourite roosts.

Autumn ▶

Autumn is the time for mammals to fatten up for the harsh days which lie ahead as temperatures drop. Roe deer cast their antlers, and start to grow new ones in velvet; garden and other dormouse species guzzle as much food as possible. White grey seal pups brave their first storms; dolphins follow fish shoals inshore; and wood mice and bank voles hoard nuts.

HEDGEHOGS

HABITATS

Although hedgehogs like woodland, scrub and cover, as their name suggests, they prefer well cropped or cut grassland to find the worms and insects which are their staple diet. Hedgehogs do not tunnel, but wrap themselves up in dense collections of leaves to form solid hibernation nests under cover, and hide breeding nests in similar retreats.

HABITS

Hedgehogs roll up in a ball with spines to protect themselves from most predators. Sometimes they have two litters, May–August, about five young, which open their eyes at two weeks, can roll up from 11 days, and are weaned by six weeks. Like shrews and moles, they lead solitary lives and are a popular mammal in gardens, fed by people. Many are run over on roads at regular crossing places.

HEDGEHOG
L 22–29 cm. These mammals crouch if wary, scent the air, run quickly, swim and climb well. Nocturnal.

Spines are erect when they roll up, and these form a sharp defence. Born with soft, white ones, dark spines soon grow between these. Fleas, ticks and lice enjoy life amongst the shafts.

ALGERIAN HEDGEHOG ▽
L 22–25cm. Light skin and hair below pale spines with gap in these on crown of head. Found on SW coasts of France and Spain.

Further eastward across △ Europe, hedgehogs develop a white chin.

PROJECT

◁ Dog, and especially cat, food with water is highly nutritious to hedgehogs, particularly in dry summers.

Garden swimming pools ▷ should always have wire mesh for hedgehogs to escape when not in use.

◁ Check any cattle grids to see if they have a ramp for hedgehogs to enter or escape by. Make one or tell your local Trust.

◁ Autumn is a time when hedgehogs look for cosy nest sites in which to hibernate: make sure your local bonfire has no hedgehogs in it.

Used in excess, slug ▷ pellets may harm larger animals, such as hedgehogs.

OBSERVING HEDGEHOGS

Most people have hedgehogs living near them, but they shun daylight, so you have to go out at dusk to watch them as they tour their territories, or attract them to your home with regular meals on a dish. Ideally, stick to tinned meat and water, but milk and bread are better than nothing. If you frighten one so that it curls up, wait silently downwind and, depending on how shy it is, you should soon see it slowly uncurl. If they catch scent or sight of you when they peep out, they will abruptly close up again. Once uncurled, they run for cover on raised legs, previously hidden under the mantle of spines.

Dogs, weasels and stoats ▲ are put off by the rolled-up position. The huge back muscle relaxes when danger is past and the animal can slip away.

Hedgehogs like building nests and may have several. Grass and leaves give thick insulation to keep out rain and frost. ▶

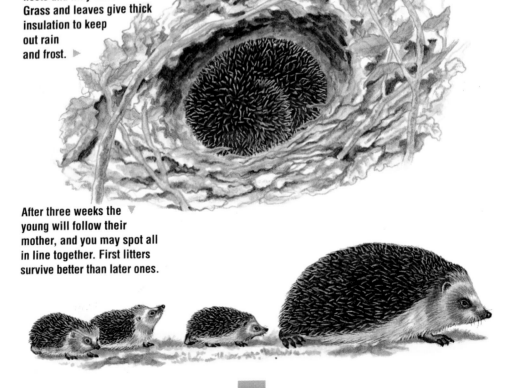

After three weeks the ▼ young will follow their mother, and you may spot all in line together. First litters survive better than later ones.

Relaxed hedgehogs snort and snuffle around after food, but in courtship they can make loud squeals. They often endlessly circle one another at this time. ▼

The black droppings on lawns or playing fields are seldom noticed unless you look carefully, and prints show up in damp ditch mud.

Hedgehogs are able to swim, although they may ▲ drown if left in garden pools.

Hedgehogs can visit many gardens, fields and woods in one night. Regular crossing places on roads result in casualties. They may curl up and freeze when they see a light, often with fatal results. ▼

◀ Even if you rescue a hedgehog from the middle of the road, they do not make good pets. Return hedgehogs to safe, covered areas.

MOLES

MOLE

L 12–15cm. Moles hunt, with tail up, at speed round tunnels. Young must leave the adult territory.

HABITATS

Moles are one of the most often noticed, yet rarest seen, mammals, because of their soil hills and tunnels just under the surface of the ground. They prefer damp woodland and pastures and, despite life in the dark, are able to open their eyes. The smaller blind mole of the Mediterranean has its eyes hidden by a membrane and lives in the drier scrub regions.

HABITS

Like shrews, moles are solitary. They eat insects and catch worms round the clock, by having four-hour activity periods when they tour their territory to see if animals have fallen into their tunnels. They sleep for three to four hours and are off again. Large 'fortress' hills usually house the one litter of three to four young, May–June.

A mole's front limbs are built for digging, with strong claws on the big feet. Their ears are hidden in their fur, their eyes are very small, and their hair flattens smoothly forward or back.

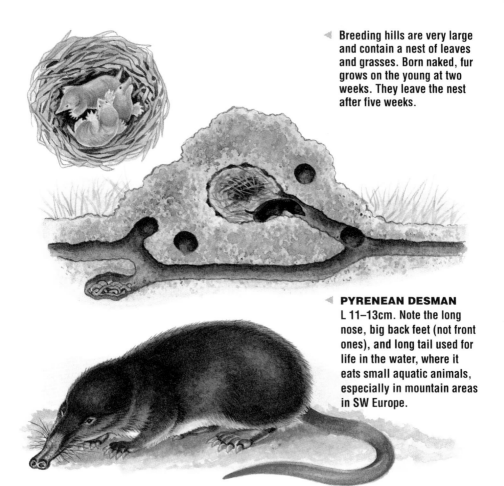

Breeding hills are very large and contain a nest of leaves and grasses. Born naked, fur grows on the young at two weeks. They leave the nest after five weeks.

◀ **PYRENEAN DESMAN**
L 11–13cm. Note the long nose, big back feet (not front ones), and long tail used for life in the water, where it eats small aquatic animals, especially in mountain areas in SW Europe.

HOW TO WATCH

Although moles are secretive and wary in their tunnels, a garden lawn well worked with tunnels is ideal for observation. Remember they alternate four-hour shifts with $3^1/2$ hours' sleep, so visit with very soft steps until you actually see movement. Worms are a good guide: they sense a mole and will panic out of the soil. When young leave you may see one on the surface 'swimming' along.

SHREWS

COMMON SHREW ▶
L 6–8cm. The most familiar shrew across Europe: tricoloured, with a long and mobile nose.

JUVENILE
The colour of the young is more uniform. The tail, when held over the body, easily reaches the back of its head.

HABITATS

You can find some sort of shrew wherever you are in Europe, from the incredibly small least species in the northern wet conifers of Scandinavia, eastwards, to the robust, black water shrews which occur in most places except the very dry regions. All the shrews have up to five litters in a year, about six young at a time, but the white-toothed have up to 10. In NE Europe there are also three other medium-sized species: Laxmann's, dusky and bicoloured white-toothed.

HABITS

Active day and night, with peaks at dawn and dusk, shrews hungrily eat insects, worms and other small creatures. They are solitary and will only tolerate others in their territory briefly to mate with. We usually hear them squeaking and softly twittering.

Shrews like to hide under a secure log or rocks, and you can put corrugated iron sheets down on grassland to see if they turn up there.

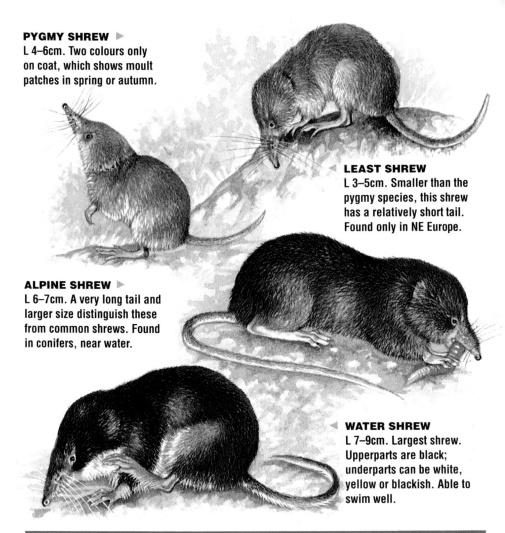

PYGMY SHREW ▷
L 4–6cm. Two colours only on coat, which shows moult patches in spring or autumn.

LEAST SHREW
L 3–5cm. Smaller than the pygmy species, this shrew has a relatively short tail. Found only in NE Europe.

ALPINE SHREW ▷
L 6–7cm. A very long tail and larger size distinguish these from common shrews. Found in conifers, near water.

WATER SHREW
L 7–9cm. Largest shrew. Upperparts are black; underparts can be white, yellow or blackish. Able to swim well.

HOW TO WATCH

Of all the shrews, a colony of water shrews gives one of the best chances of seeing these highly active mammals in the open. When a female has young it is great fun to watch them swimming and diving in a garden pool. The best way to do this is to use a hide; the simple screen type (p17) is good enough for most purposes, including long observations.

49

SHREWS

HABITATS

Shrews are most often found in hedgerows, garden borders, grassland, bracken, scrub, damp conifers, wetlands and on beaches. Their teeth split the types into two: those with red tips as if they have had a plaque test, and those which have all-white teeth. The latter also have long guard hairs on their tails and tend to live across the south of Europe, being absent from Scandinavia. Only the white-toothed shrews live on the Scilly and Channel Isles.

HABITS

White-toothed shrews are more easily watched than most if you wait by rocks on the tideline where seaweed rots and insects abound. You notice how much bigger and mobile their ears are compared with red-toothed shrews. The tail hairs stand out clearly.

Except when asleep, shrews are always active. They eat constantly and live less than two years. They are important in the diet of owls, but cats often catch shrews only to leave them uneaten.

Teeth differences ▼
Note below the teeth differences of the various shrew species – the jaws may be found in owl pellets.

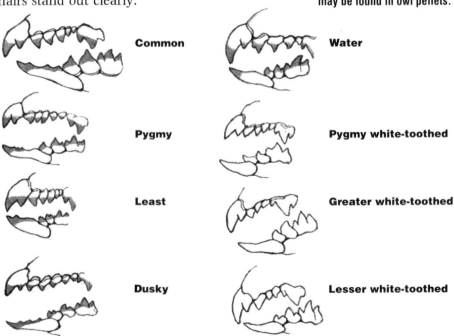

Common

Water

Pygmy

Pygmy white-toothed

Least

Greater white-toothed

Dusky

Lesser white-toothed

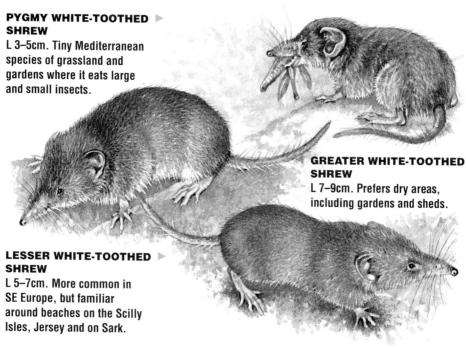

PYGMY WHITE-TOOTHED SHREW ▷
L 3–5cm. Tiny Mediterranean species of grassland and gardens where it eats large and small insects.

GREATER WHITE-TOOTHED SHREW
L 7–9cm. Prefers dry areas, including gardens and sheds.

LESSER WHITE-TOOTHED SHREW ▷
L 5–7cm. More common in SE Europe, but familiar around beaches on the Scilly Isles, Jersey and on Sark.

PROJECT

Owl pellets can be found at roosts or under favourite resting places, and shrew's skulls are easily told from one another. Note the pigment first. The analysis of teeth on the left-hand page shows the significant differences. A hand lens or illuminated binocular microscope are essential for seeing the teeth in detail for analysis.

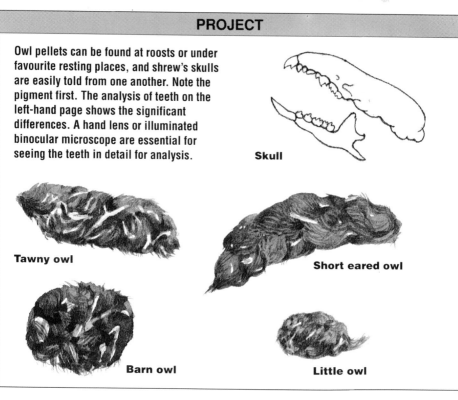

Skull

Tawny owl

Short eared owl

Barn owl

Little owl

BATS

PIPISTRELLE
Lf 2.8–3.4cm. These are small, dark bats which are one of the first on the wing at dusk. The most familiar bat seen across Europe.

HABITATS

If you stretch out your arm, extend your fingers and hold your thumb up, you can imagine how the only mammals to fly truly have adapted their limbs for flight – but, instead of feathers, their fingers are elongated and support skin as a very thin flight membrane. Equipped with a complex system of radar or echolocation (using echos to determine the position of an object) for finding their way around, bats can live in almost any habitat from towns to villages, woodlands to marsh. They must have warm, safe roost sites, and all European types hibernate.

HABITS

Roosts change from season to season. Bats choose caves, old ice houses and trees in which to hibernate. These give a constant temperature just above freezing. They feed on insects, breed in mid-summer and mate in the autumn.

Pipistrelles have adapted to warm cavity walls or hanging tiles in our homes as their normal woodland habitat has been lost and natural roosts become scarce.

LONG-EARED BAT ▷

Lf 3–4cm. One of the species active at dawn as well as after dusk, and in high summer you may even see one land on the ground to pick up a moth or spider below a street or house light. This bat will hibernate from about November to March.

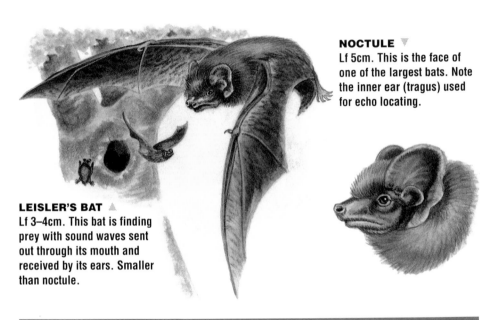

NOCTULE ▽

Lf 5cm. This is the face of one of the largest bats. Note the inner ear (tragus) used for echo locating.

LEISLER'S BAT ▲

Lf 3–4cm. This bat is finding prey with sound waves sent out through its mouth and received by its ears. Smaller than noctule.

HOW TO WATCH

Open ground near ponds and rivers is a good place to see bats at dusk through your binoculars. Insects hatch and fly from water in large numbers, attracting bats. Caves and ice houses are good places for viewing bats. Access must always be obtained through the owners' permission.

BATS

HABITS

Some species (commonly the long-eared) enter roof spaces and cling up in the apex of the rafters for warmth and safety. If you discover a roost, it must be left undisturbed, and if any work is proposed contact the Nature Conservancy Council. Roosts in houses during summer are usually all-female breeding sites because they separate from the males to have their single young together. Over 100 bats may, within days, double in number as each has its baby, but these grow quickly and usually all leave for an alternative winter roost in late summer. You can help with valuable research by counting the numbers of bats leaving the same roost from year to year. It will be even more exciting if you discover several species are present, not just one.

In lofts, droppings along the floor are easily seen on entry. Above, tucked away in warm pockets of air, are the bats. Keep water tanks well covered!

Serotines have broad ▲ wings and fly a little later in the evenings than noctules. Young are born around the end of June, and fly by August.

SEROTINE
Lf 5cm. A serotine with a juvenile on her fur. This is a large, dark-faced species.

FREE-TAILED BAT ▲
Lf 6cm. Many species migrate across Europe, and this very large bat even crosses the Alps. Note the long tail.

◁ A Natterer's colony hibernates in a hollow tree. These are medium-sized 'mouse-eared' bats and may tuck up alone in caves or underground brickwork. With eyes closed they stay inactive from about November onwards, responding only to significant changes in temperature.

TRACKER POINTS

Serotine

Whiskered

Pipistrelle

Nathusius's pipistrelle

Droppings will vary according to the size and diet of the bat and can help identify the species present. Bat groups use electronic detectors to confirm the type, too.

As the young of the year mature in the ▲ nursery colonies, they buzz with excitement and chatter as the twilight time approaches.

BATS

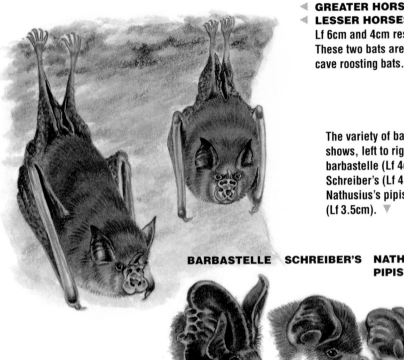

◀ **GREATER HORSEHOE BAT**
◀ **LESSER HORSESHOE BAT**
Lf 6cm and 4cm respectively. These two bats are typical of cave roosting bats.

The variety of bat heads shows, left to right: barbastelle (Lf 4cm), Schreiber's (Lf 4.5cm) and Nathusius's pipistrelle (Lf 3.5cm). ▼

BARBASTELLE   SCHREIBER'S   NATHUSIUS'S PIPISTRELLE

DECLINING NUMBERS

Bats have declined in many parts of Europe following the loss of ancient woodland, pastures and other habitats. Many wood treatments have included chemicals which kill them in our houses. Even disturbance during hibernation can be lethal: if you wake up a bat several times, it uses up its fat reserves and may die before spring.

PROTECTION OF BATS

All bats are now protected in Britain, and legislation is strict in many parts of Europe. You must apply to the Nature Conservancy Council if you want a licence to handle or photograph them.

Research under licence has told us much about the lives of bats. To stop numbering from being chewed off, light but very hard metal is put as a safe numbered band on a wing forearm, much like the ring put on a bird's leg.

DAUBENTON'S BAT ▷
POND BAT ▽
Lf 4cm and Lf 4.5cm
respectively. These bats both
fly as if to skim the surface
of water for food.

The bats shown below are
Whiskered (Lf 3.5cm),
Geoffroy's (Lf 4cm),
Natterer's (Lf 3.8cm),
Bechstein's (Lf 4.5cm) and
Brandt's (Lf 3.5cm). ▽

WHISKERED

GEOFFROY'S   **NATTERER'S**   **BECHSTEIN'S**

When in flight, bats emit ▽
very rapidly repeated sound
pulses, and these reflect off
objects as sound waves to
their ears. Bats distinguish
structures from the flying
food, which they catch and
eat. They can also see well,
and are anything but 'blind
as a bat'.

BRANDT'S

RABBITS

HABITATS

Rabbits favour grassland close to cover and are most often found where there are thickets, woods, hedgerows, sand dunes or rocky outcrops, where they can dig burrow systems. Colonies rarely stray more than 200m from their earths, although when undisturbed they will rest above ground in undergrowth.

HABITS

A doe may have litter after litter of four to six young each time. If the female is away from a burrow, she will seal the entrance with soil and grass, and only visit to feed the young.

Rabbits dig well and leave heaps of fine soil outside the entrance to a burrow. Big lumps or rocks indicate larger occupants.

RABBIT
L 33–45cm. Litters are found mostly from January to August, but young may be seen all year. Adults watch and listen carefully.

Approach colonies downwind and keep out of sight because rabbits have sharp eyes. A relaxed colony is very entertaining as bucks court does and chase off rivals, and the young play round entrances to burrows. If you are detected or a predator approaches, rabbits thump the ground with the back foot and run off, tail up.

Tracks in the snow show how the hind feet fall level, and the fore-feet print in a line, to give a very characteristic pattern as the rabbit runs. Droppings are round pellets, usually full of plant fibre. Wheat can be badly damaged by rabbits on the edge of woodland (above), and all kinds of crops are eaten or injured by them, such as cereals, roots and young trees.

HARES

HARE
L 50–65cm. Hares 'box' with their front legs during spring.

White tail underneath, with strong black top edging.
▼

Very long back legs give ▲ great speed when disturbed from hiding places. Hair hides its toes. You usually see hares running away from you, but the back of the ears show up with distinctive black tips.

HABITATS

Hares like big open spaces; flat arable land is typical. Some fields are too enclosed and may never hold hares, yet broad-leaved woods next to open land are frequently visited. Hares can be very faithful to the places where they were born, and have been known to stay all their lives in the same grassland. They love aerodromes, which are noisy but safe from predators, and have plenty of permanent grass.

HABITS

Hares do not burrow, but lie out at ground level in a shallow scrape of soil or turf called a form. Their eyes are at the top of their heads in a flattened position and, from there, they are able to see approaching danger from the front, side and rear without moving.

BLUE OR MOUNTAIN ▲
HARE
L 45–60cm. Seen here in its winter coat, it is easily visible before snow covers the ground. Although its ears are shorter than those of the brown hare, they have black tips characteristic of hares.

Grasses are the staple diet: cereals, leaves of root crops, vegetables and some bark are taken.

A shallow scrape or 'form' ▼ is favoured to allow a safe viewpoint.

HOW TO WATCH

Look in spring, especially when hares make themselves more obvious out in the middle of fields in daytime. After snowfall you can see how active the hares were overnight as paths criss-cross and mingle. Generations follow the same tracks through fences and hedges. If you regularly take a dog for walks over fields (making sure it is not a threat to livestock), it is likely to 'put up' young hares, which are less skilled at remaining hidden, or do not have access to the best retreats. They are fully grown in 240 days; but from their youth, when only half this size, they can spring sideways.

TRACKER POINTS

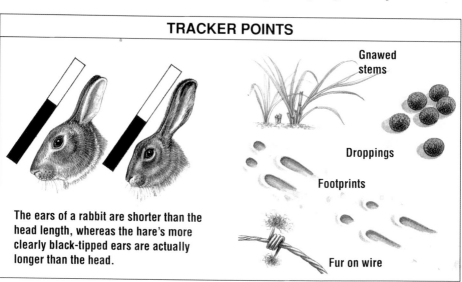

Gnawed stems

Droppings

Footprints

The ears of a rabbit are shorter than the head length, whereas the hare's more clearly black-tipped ears are actually longer than the head.

Fur on wire

RED SQUIRRELS

RED SQUIRREL
L 18–27cm. Red squirrels
prefer to eat seeds, and cut
away pine cone scales to
make it easier to get to them.

HABITATS

Squirrels can be found wherever there are trees, and the red squirrel particularly likes conifers. They are also found in broadleaved woodland, and up to 2,000m high up in mountain regions. Warm dreys are built in evergreen foliage, where one to two litters of about three young are born every year.

HABITS

Red squirrels feed up in tree canopies, but will search a litter of leaves in the autumn and, especially, in January. Food (mainly made up of seeds) is stored for winter in hollow trees or holes in the ground, and nests are made for both winter and summer.

In Europe dark, as well as red hair, varieties occur. Most have black tails, but in Britain the tail fades to pale by the spring and summer.

TRACKER POINTS

Although squirrels mostly eat in the tree canopy and leave scattered remains of stripped cones around the base, they often have favourite tree stumps where you can find scales stripped and left like litter around a picnic table. This usually occurs with conifers and deciduous trees. The top scales of a cone are usually left by squirrels. They turn the cone as they go from each scale to the next in a spiral. Squirrels cannot survive for more than a few days without eating, and many die in harsh winters if they have not been able to build up food stocks.

EUROPEAN SOUSLIK
L 17–24cm. Common to E Europe, this mammal has one litter per year, about six young. Active during day.

SPOTTED SOUSLIK
L 18–25cm. Found in E Europe. Habits similar to European, but more often seen on farmland.

ALPINE MARMOT
L 40–60cm. Large mammal, usually found on alpine pastures. Small family colonies, with one litter from the third year, about six young. Daytime animal.

GREY SQUIRRELS

GREY SQUIRREL
L 25–28cm. Squirrels are perfectly adapted to life in trees and have long back legs to allow them to leap from branch to branch at great speed.

HABITATS

In Britain, the grey squirrel is more familiar than the native red species, and is so abundant in all kinds of habitats that it is now one of the easiest mammals to watch. The squirrel will forage on the ground, visit bird tables and become tame if fed regularly by hand, in parks, gardens and public woods. They have replaced the native red squirrels in much of England and Wales, because of the nature of our mixed woodland plantations.

HABITS

Courtship chases start in January (they do not hibernate) and the first of two litters of about five young each are born in the tree dreys in spring. Tree flowers, shoots, insects, bark, nuts, orchard fruit and mast are eaten.

All kinds of acrobatics are performed to get to food put out for birds, and it is fun to watch how they evade obstacles.

Dreys are made of cut twigs on the outside, with a warm soft lining of leaves, so that damp, chill winter weather is kept out. The young are born in the drey, and in hot summer weather open, flat platform nests are built out on the tree limbs. They store nuts and acorns for the winter months by burying them.

HOW TO WATCH

Squirrels are very vocal animals, and you can often locate them by sound. Try calling back with a low 'chuck, chuck' and see if they answer. They hide on the far side of a tree, and circle round as you try to see them. They are easy to watch in bare winter tree tops, being active during the day. During autumn, they are very busy on the ground burying seeds and nuts.

TRACKER POINTS

Split nuts and footprints are easy to find in damp autumn woods, by paths and near streams.

Grey squirrels damage trees, as they gnaw the bark to get at the sapwood below.

BEAVERS

HABITATS

Beavers were once common right across Europe, and are the largest rodent living there. They are now found only in a few scattered localities, and always live in rivers or lakes with woodland close by. Although they are famous for building dams in rushing water, many live in secretive family groups in burrows on the river banks, especially where water is too wide to dam.

HABITS

Beavers have one litter in the spring of two to four young, and the mother may carry them in her mouth, supported by her arms. They are born with hair and vision and can swim and dive when very young. Beavers only eat vegetation, such as shrubs and roots.

Lodges

Beavers may build a lodge of cut branches, from young broadleaved trees like poplars, willows and aspen, with access underwater. This gives a chamber over 100cm wide by 50cm high. Mud is used to waterproof and protect the lodge: it packs down hard and keeps predators out. The young stay with the adults for a year or more.

BEAVER
L 75–100cm. There is only one rodent heavier than the beaver in the world: the 35–64kg Capybara of South America. Beavers weigh 11–30kg and can close their throats behind their tongues to gnaw wood underwater.

In parts of Scandinavia, Finland, France, Germany, Austria and Poland you may be able to locate sites by looking for felled trees, or by asking guides. A clue to finding beavers is if you hear one 'slap' the water with its tail. When one gnaws a tree, another in the family unit may keep watch close by. They favour young trees within 200m of the edge of the water. Colonies in the Rhône Valley in France show how the species can recover if protected.

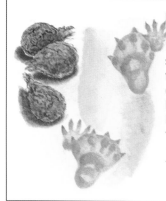

TRACKER POINTS

Beaver droppings, about 3cm long, 2cm thick, are mostly left in water but can sometimes be found on land; full of wood chips and pieces of vegetation. Beavers have big footprints, but webbing between the toes on the hind foot does not usually show up unless on soft mud. The tail partly obscures prints made in the snow.

COYPU ▲
L 40–60cm. Introduced to fur farms from S America; may be found in parts of Europe, especially France, but almost extinct in Britain. Smaller in water than the beaver, and the tail is long, without the broad rudder shape. Extensive damage done to crops and river banks by the coypu. Breeds all year, about five young.

DORMICE

HABITATS

These climbing mice nearly all have bushy tails and have facial darkening around the eyes. They all live in trees and thickets, although the mouse-tailed dormouse, which is more vole-like in looks, with a long thin tail, keeps to the ground more. They are never numerous and, being nocturnal, are hard to watch.

HABITS

Dormice run along branches and climb at speed. Hibernation is from October to April, and they construct breeding nests to have one to two litters of about five young each summer. Flowers, fruits and some animal food, especially in the case of the garden dormouse, make up their diets. All are very vocal, and fat dormice will churr angrily from branches if they see you below at night.

Oval nests are woven above the ground with twigs and cut stems. The dormice line the inside with soft leaves, or seed heads.

PROJECT

Nest boxes for dormice to shelter or breed in help these rare mammals, and you can build them in wood or design your own, using a plastic drainpipe and wooden plugs. Local Trusts may organise workshops which you can join.

FAT DORMOUSE ▽
L 12–20cm. These mice are large and grey, with a bushy tail. Also called the edible dormouse.

◀ **GARDEN DORMOUSE**
L 10–18cm. Big ears, 'bandit' mask and tufted tip on a long tail, describe these mice. Not shy to enter houses and gardens, they are also elusive and nocturnal.

FOREST DORMOUSE ▷
L 7–13cm. Like hazel dormice, these mice prefer broadleaf woodland with thickets. Nest high in trees.

LEMMINGS AND HAMSTERS

NORWAY LEMMING
L 13–15cm. Lives on the
plant life of Scandinavia, and
sports bright colours.

HABITATS

Although lemmings look much the same as
voles (but with even shorter tails and, apart
from the grey wood lemming, brighter colours),
hamsters have distinctly bigger ears and huge
cheek pouches to collect seeds for storage. They
live in grassland, scrub or forest and make
complex burrows in which they move from
nest to feeding sites, out of view of predators as
much as possible. Lemmings are typical of the
north and stay active, even breeding under the
snow. Hamsters store food and hibernate.

HABITS

Norway lemmings are famous for migrating to
find fresh pasture every few years when their
populations build up to points of conflict. All
have litters of about four young, and their
surface runways show up particularly clearly
after snow has melted.

WOOD LEMMING ▲
L 8–10cm. Lives and feeds
on moss under conifers in N
and E Europe. Distinguished
by a red line on its grey back.

COMMON HAMSTER
L 21–32cm. This is a large, attractively coloured rodent. Has about two litters of about 10 young per year.

GOLDEN HAMSTER
L 17–18cm. Prefers to live in dry grassland and cornfields. Breeds of various shades and is a popular pet.

GREATER MOLE RAT
L 19–30cm (lesser mole rat L 15–27cm). These rodents live underground, eating roots and plants. They have one litter per year, of about five young.

MUSKRAT
L 26–40cm. Twice the size of the water vole, found in N America, C and N Europe. Several litters per year with about eight young.

PORCUPINE
L 60–80cm. Long spines for defence. Usually one litter per year, of about four young. Old quills are found outside their burrows.

VOLES

HABITATS

Voles are one of our most abundant small mammals, particularly across the lush vegetation areas of North and Central Europe. There is a vole species to gnaw vegetation at every level: below ground, the pine vole likes roots and bulbs; at ground level, field voles feed on grasses, and into the shrub and tree canopy the bank voles will take fruits and nuts.

HABITS

All species breed rapidly, do not hibernate and have activity periods around the clock. These mammals are preyed upon by large birds of prey and any mammal or bird big enough to kill them. Their breeding period is usually March–October.

Nests are approached by ▲ well-hidden but worn paths. They have escape runs and paths to latrines nearby.

BANK VOLE
L 8–12cm. Hair tends to be longer than in mice, with a shaggy look and less athletic. Red-brown on back.

The lips of a bank vole are pink, and its whiskers are 2cm long. ▼

Note shorter tail than in mice. (In field vole it is half this length, and very thin in the pine vole.)

Ears are less obvious than in mice and more flat to the side of the head, almost hidden by hair in the grass voles.

Juvenile field voles ▷
in a typically simple chewed
grass nest, which is usually
found at the centre of an
inter-connecting system of
burrows. All of the 20 types
of small voles in Europe
have offspring which can
breed in a few weeks and
have several litters of about
five young each time, from
spring to autumn.

◁ **PINE VOLE**
◁ **BANK VOLE**
A pine vole (L 8–10cm), far
left, compared with a field
vole (L 8–13cm): the pine
vole has smaller eyes, ears
and feet, with neater hair and
a thinner tail. Both are
herbivorous, feeding on
stems and leaves; and both
prefer to live on damp
meadows and open
woodlands.

TRACKER POINTS

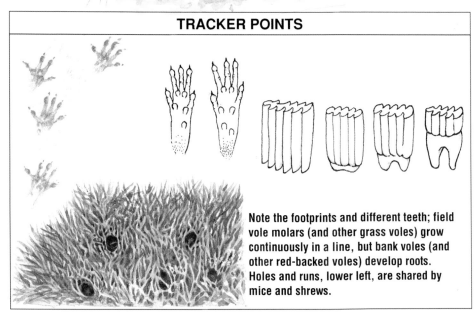

Note the footprints and different teeth; field
vole molars (and other grass voles) grow
continuously in a line, but bank voles (and
other red-backed voles) develop roots.
Holes and runs, lower left, are shared by
mice and shrews.

WATER VOLES

WATER VOLE
L 12–21cm. Water voles are normally to be found throughout Europe.

HABITATS

If you walk quietly along the bank of almost any river, canal or backwater, the 'plop' of a water vole as it dives out of sight will betray its presence. Burrows have underwater access and are built where sedges, grasses and other bankside marsh plants provide shelter.

HABITS

A stream of bubbles shows where one is swimming. Although large, they share the common vole features of blunt nose, small ears and rough coat. Those that avoid predators such as herons and mink may live up to two years. Nests are woven in marsh plants and up to five litters of about five young are born in March–October, depending upon conditions. The juveniles leave the nest when half grown, so you may see a variety of sizes.

Distinguish from a swimming rat (lower picture) by the distinct wake of water ripples, high rear end, flattened ears and rounded nose of the vole.

Look for worn mud paths where pieces of grass (a water vole's main diet) are left, and throw fresh cut apples as close as possible to them. Wait silently downwind and, with luck, the voles will emerge to feed. Watch a water vole swim, holding its blunt nose clear of the water, and making a V-shaped wave as it paddles with all four legs.

Tunnels are made into ▷ river banks without causing much damage, and have holes which allow hidden escapes into the water. The first signs are usually droppings near the tunnels; these are cylindrical, 1cm long, pale brown or green.

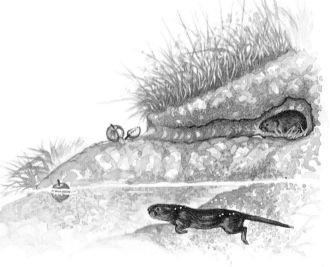

◁ **SOUTH-WESTERN WATER VOLE**
L 20cm. In Spain, Portugal and France look for this larger vole, which is darker and has a longer tail. While the northern water vole may dig burrows remote from water, this species is never far from river or lake edges.

RATS

BROWN RAT
L 18–26cm. Note the stout body and thick tail of the adult.

HABITATS

Both black and brown rats spread into Europe from Asia and are associated with human trade routes. They colonize buildings, outhouses and shipping. Common rats are found almost everywhere that people live or work and, although both species are nocturnal, they can become active in daylight and quite bold if left undisturbed. Both can transmit disease to humans by contamination of water and be carriers of bubonic plague. (The ship rat transmitted this 'Black Death' via its fleas in Europe during the Middle Ages.) Ship rats are more associated with ports and shipping.

HABITS

Black rats keep to ships and buildings, but common rats burrow extensively and use pathways. Both store food and can breed all year, about seven young per litter.

Barn owls have always helped farmers reduce rat populations. Stoats, weasels, polecats and foxes are other predators, which catch mainly young rats.

Old grain stores were built on top of pillars in the shape of mushrooms to keep rats out. They climb well but cannot pass the overhang. Black rats easily navigate ropes onto ships, so many are fitted with blocks to prevent their passage.

BLACK RAT ▲
L 16–23cm. Obvious, hairless ears, and guard hairs above rest of coat. Long tapering tail. Variable colour.

TRACKER POINTS

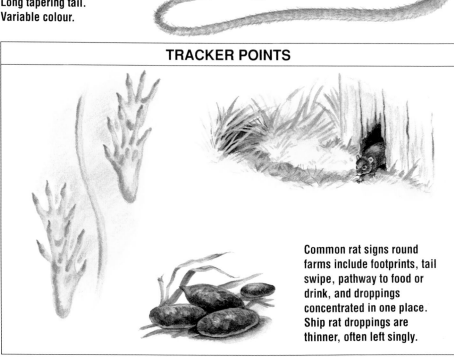

Common rat signs round farms include footprints, tail swipe, pathway to food or drink, and droppings concentrated in one place. Ship rat droppings are thinner, often left singly.

MICE

WOOD MOUSE
L 11cm. These mice are
territorial and may fight.
Litters May–October, about
six young. Nocturnal.

HABITATS

Mice have adapted to every major type of
habitat. The two most commonly found are
wood mice, throughout Europe (apart from the
very cold north of Scandinavia), and house
mice, associated with human buildings and
food stores virtually everywhere. Most live in
burrows with warm nests, and leave to feed at
night, but harvest mice (pp 82–3) construct
homes for their young in tall vegetation above
the ground.

HABITS

Like voles and lemmings, mice are small,
abundant, gnawing mammals (rodents) which
eat all kinds of vegetable matter. Some eat
insects and others store big heaps of grain. All
breed rapidly and can move very fast, often
jumping out of danger with a series of springs
of their powerful back legs. Bright eyes, big ears
and long tails are characteristic.

**Mice groom, like all land
mammals, to keep their fur
healthy, but when nervous
they will also wash as a
means of calming
themselves down.**

YELLOW-NECKED MOUSE
L 9–12 cm. Larger than the wood mouse, with a yellow chest band. Lives in woodland, hedgerows and gardens.

STRIPED FIELD MOUSE
L 7–12cm. These mice are found in E Europe, under light canopy habitats. They have about five litters a year.

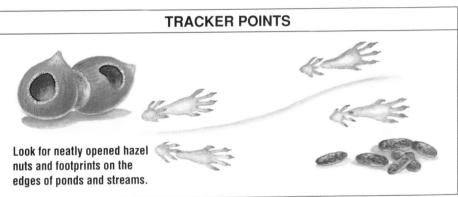

TRACKER POINTS

Look for neatly opened hazel nuts and footprints on the edges of ponds and streams.

ROCK MOUSE ▷
L 8–15cm. This mouse is the largest of the field mouse species. Grey or sandy coloured with white underparts, it lives on rocky hillsides and thorn scrub. They have to be wary of all kinds of birds of prey, especially owls, which hunt in the half-light as well as in total darkness.

MICE

HABITATS

House mice have followed humans all round the world to every locality, and all kinds of other pet mice have been bred from them. Their origins are in E Europe, possibly the Mediterranean, too. They became the most valuable and most often bred animal (alongside rats) for medical research. Similar species are the Algerian mouse, found on farms and gardens, and the northern birch mouse, typical of the birch woodland in NE Europe.

Some larders seem to attract generation after generation of house mice which scent food and enter through ducting or gaps in brickwork.

HABITS

Mice make complicated runs and burrows which they get to know well. They all differ in small ways: certain spiny mice shed their tails easily, like lizards; birch mice eat more insects than seeds, and hibernate.

HOUSE MOUSE
L 9cm. When natural bedding is hard to find, house mouse mothers will chew up paper, linen or plastic to use as a nest.

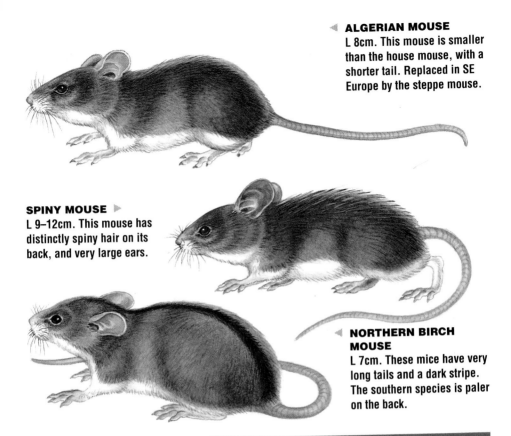

ALGERIAN MOUSE
L 8cm. This mouse is smaller than the house mouse, with a shorter tail. Replaced in SE Europe by the steppe mouse.

SPINY MOUSE ▷
L 9–12cm. This mouse has distinctly spiny hair on its back, and very large ears.

NORTHERN BIRCH MOUSE
L 7cm. These mice have very long tails and a dark stripe. The southern species is paler on the back.

HOW TO WATCH

Cats, wild or domestic, teach us much about how to watch. They catch small mammals by patience and a quick pounce (below).

Mouse activity peaks at dawn and dusk (above), so that the more you are out watching animals, the more you may see mice emerge from fox, badger or rabbit earths, or climb down twigs.

HARVEST MICE

The harvest mouse is the smallest rodent in Europe. Although its long prehensile tail is very mouse-like, its ears are rather hidden, like those of the grass vole. Harvest mice make beautiful woven nests of living grasses by chewing long thin leaves into strips without killing the plant, and then plaiting them into a strong, cosy sphere the size of a tennis ball. You can, in fact, fix a tennis ball with a small hole in the side on top of a 50cm high wooden post as a nest-box in wetland to help watch the mice. The young will eat their way out of the nest in less than three weeks. Look for nests in marshy places, by country roads, ditches and on hedges and corn crops before harvest.

When they lose their nest site, the mice retreat to the permanent marginal habitat in grassland and thickets.

HARVEST MOUSE
L 7cm. Harvest mice climb easily, using their tail as a fifth limb. They live in winter nests on the ground, but may spend the summer on stems above standing marsh water.

As more mice are bred, ▷ the colonies spread out from wetland into standing corn, hence the name.

◁ Sometimes populations build up to large colonies. As the mice run away, they show the red fur on their little backs clearly.

They feed on insects as ▽ well as seeds and fruits. During their courtship (May–September), the individuals may fight, and there is also aggression as the young are forced to disperse.

If you find a complete ⌂ nest, sit and watch and you may see the mother push out or approach to feed the five or so young.

STOATS

STOAT

L 17–32cm. The young stoats can stay with their mother for several months, learning about hunting live animals.

The female will catch a young rabbit, and take it back to feed the hungry family as they are weaned off her milk.

HABITATS

Stoats are able to live in all kinds of habitats but, unlike weasels, are not found in the Mediterranean. They prey mainly on smaller mammals and birds, but regularly take rabbits, which are much larger than they are; so they need to have a territory which includes a plentiful supply of animals to catch.

HABITS

They have six to 12 young in early summer, and these can stay to hunt with the mother until the autumn, hence the description of a 'pack' of stoats. The long tail has a black tip, and this can distract birds of prey as they try to catch the stoats. You may notice a stoat run and flick its tail as it escapes from view.

When they leave the nest, the young are already fit from play-fighting. Scaling walls is not a difficult task for them.

TRACKER POINTS

Footprints show up in soft ground.
Droppings c 8mm long, 5mm in diameter.

Males are larger than females, but ▲
stoats change to ermine (white in winter,
leaving a black tail tip), usually across N
Europe. Ermine fur was prized for trimming
ceremonial robes, the distinct black tail tips
being left on the gown for show.

Stoats are always curious ▶
and will usually re-appear if
disturbed. They look into any
crevices or runs and are
easily trapped. You can call
them by 'squeaking' on the
back of your hand because
they think you are an injured
rabbit. They help farmers by
keeping the numbers of
rodents and rabbits down.

▼ Stoats swim readily, but may
be driven off by angry parent
birds which defend their
nests on islands.

FOXES

RED FOX

L 50–80cm. At dawn or dusk you may see a fox tracking and catching a small mammal by scent or sight. They become tense, and then spring in an arc onto the mouse or vole.

HABITATS

Although the red fox is found in all parts of Europe, it is shy and difficult to watch. This is due to its acute senses and fear of humans, having been persecuted for rabies control in Europe, hunted for sport and shot or trapped by gamekeepers. Primarily a woodland predator adapted to farmland, moorland, gardens and even towns. Arctic foxes live in the far north and feed on small mammals, birds and eggs.

HABITS

An average of five, often ten or more, cubs are born in one spring litter, after a noisy January courtship with much barking and scream-like calls. As well as eating small mammals, birds, worms, fruits, insects and carrion, they will eat human food waste.

Fox coats are very varied, but there are three main colour types: the red-brown one shown here, which is typical of Europe; a black type known as silver; and a cross form, red and black.

WOLF
L 105–160cm. The wolf is still present in E Europe but few are seen elsewhere. Three to five cubs are born in one litter per year.

JACKAL ▷
L 70–100cm. Found in SE Europe only, very shy. About five cubs per litter, each year (born underground).

RED FOX
L 50–80cm. Pointed nose, sharp ears, black on legs and bushy, white-tipped tail. Runs fast, strong scent.

RACCOON DOG ▲
L 65–80cm. This mammal has a mask like a raccoon and legs like a dog. Found in NE Europe only.

TRACKER POINTS

Dog

Fox

Footprints in straight lines in snow; round pads leave fine nail and hair prints; droppings have pointed ends.

ARCTIC FOX ▲
L 45–65cm. Moults from brown into thick white winter coat.

FOXES

Safe, dry underground ▼
earths are chosen by a vixen
to have her cubs, and the dog
fox helps feed her.

GENERAL FEATURES

In spring, vixens select secluded earths in
which to breed. Cubs start life with thin
chocolate brown coats and are blind until two
weeks old. At first their eyes open as pale blue,
but they gradually change to deep yellow as
their fur becomes brown, and they develop a
light grey chest by eight weeks.

**Three-week cub,
still underground**

**Outside earth, four
to five weeks**

OBSERVATION

To watch fox cubs, keep at least 10m from the
earth, well hidden downwind so that the vixen
does not become alarmed. When she leaves or
returns, she may give a sharp warning bark if
she thinks a human is nearby. Arctic fox cubs
can be watched in the constant daylight of
their summer, but the dens of wolves, raccoon-
dogs and jackals in NE or SE Europe require
local guides or wardens to direct you.

**Playful and curious
at eight weeks**

Although adult foxes are very wary, they will come to food which is put out every night at the same place, and will get used to seeing artificial lights. Cubs are very tame in the first few days of their emergence at the entrance to the earth, but parents may move them if they scent that you have been too close.

◀ The courtship of foxes takes place in the darkest months of the year as they follow each other, compete, and play, during December and early January. The vixen is receptive to the dog fox for just three days, and you may be lucky enough to see them together on a sunny January morning after much overnight barking.

Fox-hunting with hounds ▷ is a traditional sport, made fashionable over the last 200 years. Hounds scent through cover and, when a fox is disturbed, they chase it until they either catch and kill it or lose the scent. Earths and badger setts are blocked to stop them escaping into the ground. If they go to earth, terriers kill them underground, or they are dug out and killed. An aniseed scent trail carried by a terrier can be used instead.

WEASELS

HABITATS

Absent only from Ireland, the weasel can be found throughout Europe in every type of habitat, and is the smallest carnivore present. It is small enough to hunt into mouse or vole runs, but will also climb to take birds and eggs in a nest.

You may find a simple nest under logs where a weasel has taken over from a mouse or vole and likes the site. It may have eaten the mouse or vole first!

HABITS

Weasels have one or two litters each year of four to six young. Like all predators they have very alert senses and, although they may see or scent you on a path, if you wait silently they usually return to look at you before going on their way. They chatter very loudly and issue strong scent if at all frightened. When threatened, they hiss and lunge at the cause of their concern. They are active both during the day and at night.

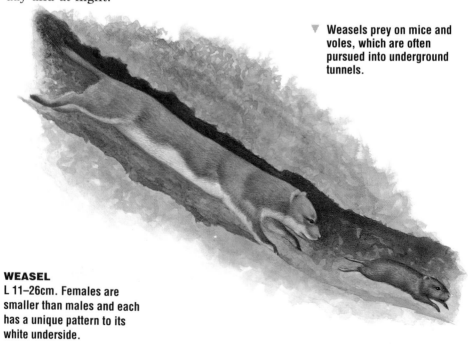

▽ Weasels prey on mice and voles, which are often pursued into underground tunnels.

WEASEL
L 11–26cm. Females are smaller than males and each has a unique pattern to its white underside.

TRACKER POINTS

Weasel tracks are hard to find and look smudged in snow, but tiny pads sometimes show in very soft mud. Droppings are thin, tapering, up to 6mm long, 3mm in diameter. Territories are marked using musk secreted from the anal glands.

Weasels have long, slender bodies and  short limbs. They are alert mammals, frequently sitting upright to look around and smell the air for prey.

WOLVERINE
L 70–100cm. Scandinavia and Finland. Three young in spring. Nocturnal; largest of the weasel family.

EGYPTIAN MONGOOSE
L 45-60cm. S Spain and Portugal. Two to four in a litter. Active during the day; occasionally at night.

GENET
L 40–60cm. France, Iberia. Two to three in litter. Nocturnal.

MINK

HABITATS

Mink look black at a distance but have a soft, very dark brown coat and white chin. The European species is now rather rare in the East with a small population in W France. American mink have escaped from fur farms and are found in Britain, France, Scandinavia and parts of E Europe. Both live along river valleys, lakes and in marshland, feeding on fish, amphibians, water voles, muskrats, and water birds.

HABITS

Mink have one litter of four or five young each year in hollow trees or burrows near water, and these grow in much the same way as polecats, but are introduced to swimming and disperse along the valleys and watercourses before the autumn. Will purr and scream in play or fight.

Pastel mink of grey or brown are found captive in fur farms. Wild mink gradually breed back to the original brown, but you may spot colour varieties.

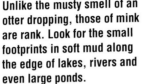

Unlike the musty smell of an otter dropping, those of mink are rank. Look for the small footprints in soft mud along the edge of lakes, rivers and even large ponds.

The European mink (top) has white on the muzzle and chin. White is confined to the chin in the bigger American species.

The mink's hair has excellent insulation, even when it is wet. Fresh out of the water, the hairs go spiky, but this is soon dried and grooms to a silky gloss, which is why the mink's fur became popular for making coats, and why so many fur farms have been established. Escaped mink have bred in the wild since the 1950s.

Although they catch many fish, water voles are a favourite prey for mink, which chase them from river-bank tunnels. They are small enough to hunt into burrows where otters would be unable to go.

MARTENS AND POLECATS

HABITATS

Pine martens and beech martens are nimble, long-tailed woodland predators, which also enjoy fruits and berries. They were once found in most countries, but have become rare or absent in places, as have polecats, which eat all kinds of animal food.

HABITS

The martens climb and may nest above ground (one litter of three young), but usually spring or bound along established pathways. You can detect their presence by finding droppings or by listening for alarm calls from birds as they move about in cover, but all three species tend to be nocturnal. Polecats (one litter of about eight young) climb well, but hunt mostly on the ground, and have a distinct pungent scent.

Martens may nest up in ivy on trees, and their droppings are freely left on rocks and at junctions of paths.

PINE MARTEN
L 38–59cm. Very agile in trees as well as on the ground, they use their tails for balance.

Female polecats select a hidden den in rocks, or a burrow in which to have their young. The kittens are weaned by two months, and eat animals brought back to the nest. They are able to hunt and pounce on small mammals by this time. They practice this in play and also mount each other, chewing at their play-mate's neck.

MARTENS AND POLECATS ▷

Martens and polecats have similar heads with small ears and long, thin bodies. Note the patterns: pine marten (L 38–59cm), beech marten (L 38–48cm), marbled polecat (L 27–38cm), steppe polecat (L 32–56cm), face of polecat (black or dark chocolate brown body) (L 31–48cm), and face of domestic form, the ferret (L 40cm).

PINE   **BEECH**   **MARBLED**

STEPPE   **POLECAT**   **FERRET**

Polecat kittens are born with a thin covering of white hair, and are blind for the first five weeks or so. Their hair darkens to adult black or dark brown coats with cream underfur. By eight weeks they play vigorously, and males are heavier, with thick necks, wide heads and big feet. They chatter and scream if they are startled.

BADGERS

BADGER
L 60–90cm. Cubs are very playful, as with other members of the weasel family (stoats, polecats, martens, mink and otters).

HABITATS

Badgers have distinctive black and white faces, with broad bodies on powerful short legs. They live in colonies, underground, throwing out obvious heaps of soil at the entrances to their tunnels, and emerge to forage at dusk. Hilly districts on the borders of woods or thickets, with easily worked soils, are preferred right across Europe, except in the north of Scandinavia.

HABITS

The colonies feed on earthworms and other small animals, fruits, cereals and vegetables, using well-worn paths to favourite pastures or clearings. In the dry Mediterranean hills, insects predominate in the diet. As with all wild mammals, road accidents are a major cause of death. They are also deliberately persecuted by some humans.

Badgers take care to keep their setts warm and clean. Damp bedding is thrown out, and fresh, dry grass or straw is scratched up and gathered in armfuls.

The size of a badger territory will depend upon how much food is available round the year. This aerial view has the territories plotted on top. The colony defends the area in which it lives, but an individual may leave and start up a new colony, or join existing ones from time to time. Disputes can be noisy, with loud screams and whickering. Scars above the tail and chewed ears are quite common.

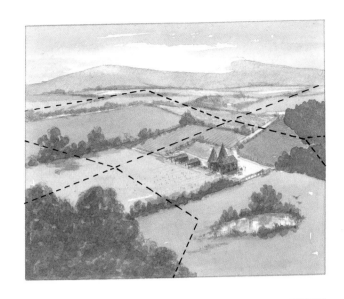

TRACKER POINTS

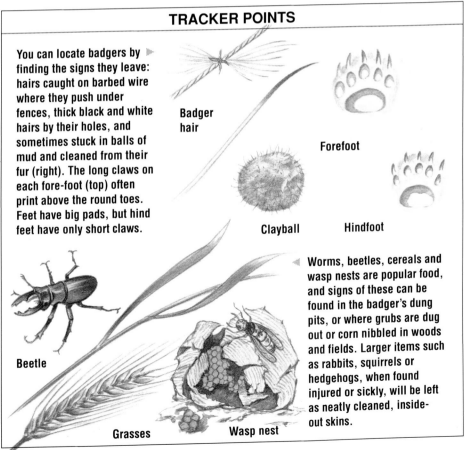

You can locate badgers by finding the signs they leave: hairs caught on barbed wire where they push under fences, thick black and white hairs by their holes, and sometimes stuck in balls of mud and cleaned from their fur (right). The long claws on each fore-foot (top) often print above the round toes. Feet have big pads, but hind feet have only short claws.

Badger hair

Forefoot

Clayball

Hindfoot

Beetle

Grasses

Wasp nest

Worms, beetles, cereals and wasp nests are popular food, and signs of these can be found in the badger's dung pits, or where grubs are dug out or corn nibbled in woods and fields. Larger items such as rabbits, squirrels or hedgehogs, when found injured or sickly, will be left as neatly cleaned, inside-out skins.

BADGERS

Badger-watching is in many ways just like going to the theatre, but nothing is planned and you must never let your scent drift towards the sett. They love woodland edges with cover round the earths, and may live for generations in main breeding setts with subsidiary, annexed or outlying groups of holes within their territory. They have a 'pecking order' of dominance in their colonies which can number up to six, ten or more in places. They are active all year round, but very quiet in December and January in the north of Europe.

Scratched trees ▶
Trees scratched by its claws are often found near the badger's sett.

◀ When watching at the sett keep 10m or so from the soil heaps where you expect to see the badgers. As well as having the wind blowing from the sett to you, wear drab clothes, shade your face and hands, and keep quiet and still.

Sett entrance ◀
Tunnel entrances take on the smooth rounded outline of the occupants.

Mound of earth ▲
As one of nature's great diggers, the badger throws out mounds of soil which can become huge over the years.

Sleeping chamber ▲
There may be a number of sleeping chambers, one of which is likely to be near the sett entrance.

Dung pits ▲
Badgers scrape soil pits for their latrines and use them for territorial scents.

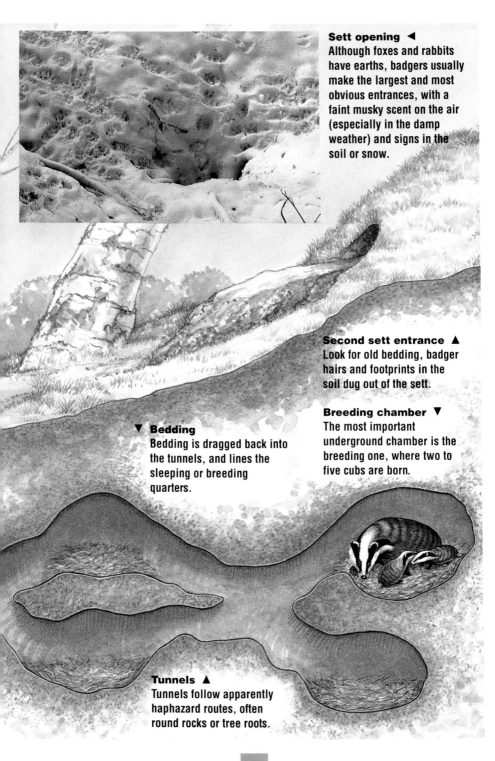

Sett opening ◄
Although foxes and rabbits have earths, badgers usually make the largest and most obvious entrances, with a faint musky scent on the air (especially in the damp weather) and signs in the soil or snow.

Second sett entrance ▲
Look for old bedding, badger hairs and footprints in the soil dug out of the sett.

Breeding chamber ▼
The most important underground chamber is the breeding one, where two to five cubs are born.

▼ Bedding
Bedding is dragged back into the tunnels, and lines the sleeping or breeding quarters.

Tunnels ▲
Tunnels follow apparently haphazard routes, often round rocks or tree roots.

OTTERS

OTTER
L 60–90cm. Note the long,
tapering tail and small ears.
They have a loud whistle,
sharp bark and growl.

Otters eat numerous eels
in a year, and catch fish,
crustaceans (such as
crayfish) and water insects.

HABITATS

Otters have become very rare across
Europe in the last 30 years, largely as a
result of chemicals being washed into
rivers from farming or industrial activities
by humans. They were once present around
the coasts, lakes, marshes, rivers and streams
throughout Europe, but are now found
only in a few, remote unpolluted places;
they are now protected by law.

HABITS

These are shy, nocturnal carnivores which are
beautifully adapted to swimming and hunting
for food in and around water. They were hard
to watch even when common on rivers because
of their nocturnal activity and shy behaviour,
due to persecution, before they became a
protected species. They give birth to one litter
of two or three cubs, usually in spring. They
feed on all kinds of aquatic and marsh species
of fish, birds and mammals.

Just like other members of
the weasel family, otters
bound along river banks and
swim with ease (using their
webbed feet).

Otters like plenty of cover near quiet, fresh water, though they may be seen crossing open land. Cubs have a piping call and whicker. On the coasts they eat crabs in large numbers, and their activity will follow the tides, rather than darkness. The young otters will stay with their mother for about a year. Territories are likely to be marked with droppings and scent, and the otters may range over seven km or more of rivers.

TRACKER POINTS

Estuary mud is good for finding the distinct toes and pad prints of otters. Musk-scented droppings of food remains are left on prominent rocks and mounds. Look also for steep muddy – or snowy – banks used as slides for games by otter families.

Underwater, otters close ⚠ their ears and nose, but use eyes and whiskers to capture fish. Rivers and lakes free of pollution are needed to preserve otters.

WILD CATS

HABITATS

Wild cats have been forced by persecution to live in remote mountain forest areas and survive in parts of S and C Europe, with a slowly recovering population in Scotland. They lie up in dens under fallen trees, amongst rocks or in vacated burrows.

HABITS

Three to five young are usually born after a 65-day gestation in one litter during May. The kittens will play at the entrance to their den like fox cubs when a few weeks old, and hunt on their own by the autumn. They are shy, nocturnal animals and stay alone except during courtship in early spring.

One way to distinguish between the domestic and wild cat, is to look at the tail shape, which is thicker and blunt-ended in the wild cat.

WILD CAT ▲
L 45–65cm. Kittens are weaned into an adult diet of small mammals, hares, rabbits, birds and amphibians.

Domestic cats (right) are half the size of wild cats, with thin tapered tails. Note the face and tail of the lynx (L 80–130cm) and the raccoon (L 50–60cm), found locally in parts of Europe.

TABBY CAT

LYNX

RACCOON

TRACKER POINTS

Droppings often left in obvious places, are about 20x2cm, strongly scented; footprint shows as four toes and oval pad.

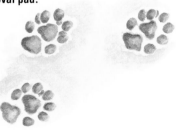

Second litters may indicate interbreeding with domestic cats where wild cats live near human habitation. The kittens are weaned by five months, and learn hunting skills in play.

103

COMMON SEALS

HABITATS

Common seals prefer sandy estuaries, fiords and rocky inlets away from the full force of the open sea. The species is found in the N Pacific and Atlantic Oceans, with one of the widest distributions of all seals. Although they live and feed in the water, they still haul out on the shore to breed and to moult their hair. At these times you can watch them on the NW coasts of Europe.

Common seals haul out on sand in places, and make very impressive flipper prints beside the body furrow.

HABITS

Diet includes all kinds of seafoods: fish, shellfish, crabs and lobsters. A single pup is born around June, and this can swim with its mother at once. Adults moult over three weeks around August, at which time specialists can monitor seal numbers by approaching downwind and out of sight.

The seal pup's eyes are ▲ open from birth. It lost its white fur shortly after it was born, and suckles from its mother on the shore.

COMMON SEAL
L 160–200cm. The common seal will often live in shallow waters, frequently in groups numbering several hundred.

As well as crawling along  estuary gullies with a guide in order to view seals hauled-out in August, you can watch them on rocks from boats in places. Never approach so close that you frighten them, especially when pups are present. Males will rise up and crash on to the water surface if they see you as a threat.

Fish are caught in the ▷ mouth by speed and skill. Some are held in the claws of the flippers to be eaten in several stages.

MONK SEAL ▽
L 230–300cm. Has one autumn pup in a cave. Only seal species in the Mediterranean. Only about 500 are left.

GREY SEALS

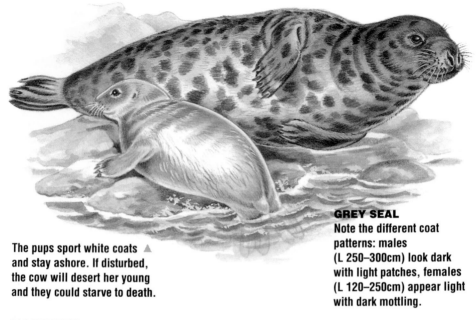

The pups sport white coats ▲ and stay ashore. If disturbed, the cow will desert her young and they could starve to death.

HABITATS

Grey seals keep to the open seas off NW Europe and breed in the autumn on exposed rocky islands. They haul themselves on to rocks or beaches to moult in the spring, and then return to the seas.

Grey seal

Common seal

Monk seal

HABITS

One pup is born around October when the cows have chosen a safe part of the traditional breeding areas. The mother will feed only her own pup, and scents it carefully at birth to fix on the one offspring. Five or so times each day the pup suckles for 10 minutes, and doubles its birth weight in a week. After a month of rapid growth, the mother leaves to mate with one or more bulls. The pup enters the sea to fend for itself. They eat sand eels, cod and many other types of fish.

Profiles of grey, common and monk seals. Other vagrant seals rarely leave their Arctic waters.

Watching grey seals is best done from cliffs above their breeding or moulting sites, where you will not disturb them. Be very quiet, and use binoculars to see the different colours and sizes of the animals. They mix freely with common seals in places and, although larger, are difficult to distinguish when bobbing about in the water. Grey seals have widely-spaced nostrils and the males are much larger than the females. The bulls seem very clumsy as they move about on the shore.

▼ Bull grey seals develop huge necks and shoulders, and fight each other for groups of cows to mate with at breeding time. If fights develop, you may see deep bite marks on their necks. Few bulls will survive beyond the age of 20.

WILD BOARS

HABITATS

Wild boar were the species from which all our varieties of domestic pig were bred, and their natural home is broadleaved woodland. When you see free-range pigs on farms foraging into the soil, it is just the same way the wild boar seek out food in the woods. Widespread across Europe, but no longer found in Britain.

HABITS

Boars, with striking, sharp tusks, live alone except when courting sows in the winter. Family groups will stay together in deep cover and feed out during the day or the night. The piglets have stripes, and you may see the product of two litters still living together. They feed on all kinds of animal, as well as vegetable, food.

WILD BOAR
L 120–200cm. Note the prominent snout and tusks on this heavy wild boar. Hunted in places, and dangerous if cornered.

No other hoofed mammal in Europe has a nest: although simple, it does serve to protect the striped piglets for the first few days of life. Their markings slowly grow out as they learn to explore with their mother.

Boar are very shy, but you can track them, and may find wallows in damp areas where they have enjoyed a cool mud bath. They are active in daytime as well as at night, but are very shy and defensive if they feel threatened. You may mistake domestic pig footprints in the forest because these animals are sometimes turned out to be fattened up before slaughter in various districts.

Piglets suckle from their mother as she lies on her side. They will wean from milk onto the adult food of acorns, beech mast, bulbs, roots, worms and beetles: a true omnivore, eating all types of food available. They will also visit farm fields, and help themselves to crops such as potatoes. Wild boar also enjoy wallowing in mud as part of a group (left).

MOUFLON, IBEXES & CHAMOIS

MOUFLON
L 120–150cm. A male
mouflon nimbly negotiates
rocky terrain. Males graze in
groups, apart from the adult
females, until the rut.

ALPINE IBEX

SPANISH IBEX

WILD GOAT

HABITATS

Both the native and domestic sheep and goats
of Europe are masters of high, rocky ground,
where people easily stumble and trip. Mouflon
are wild sheep found on mountains or
woodland around the Mediterranean, C and S
Europe. Alpine ibex and Spanish ibex are goats
with horns in both sexes, which are especially
long in the Alpine species, who live high in
mountain areas. Chamois are also goats where
both sexes grow horns, and are found locally
on high mountain sides in C Europe in
summer, or in forests during winter months.

HABITS

All have autumn or winter ruts, and have their
young in the spring. Food includes grasses,
lichens, sedges, scrub and, like deer, they
browse trees for leaves and twigs.

Chamois live in groups and need to be approached carefully from downwind to observe. In summer, they are a light brown colour, and the young kids will play-butt each other as they gambol on the alpine slopes. You are less likely to see the males at this time because they tend to be solitary in the summer. As in all mammal watching, remember to take insect-repellant with you!

Mouflon (right) have long ▷ curved horns in the male, but these are tiny or missing in the female. Alpine ibex (L 115–170cm) have high-standing horns with lumps on the front surface, and lack the chocolate-brown colouring of the mouflon. Spanish ibex (L 100–140cm) horns sweep back into an upward curve, whilst wild goat horns curve over in an even line.

CHAMOIS ▷
L 90–140cm. In winter, chamois grow a dark brown coat. They can raise the hair along their backs to threaten each other, and may look very rough-coated in this pose. They have a backward hook on the top of their horns. Chamois are endangered in all European mountain ranges because of man, tourism and increasing winter sports.

ROE DEER

HABITATS

Roe deer live by browsing or grazing on vegetation in and around woodlands right across Europe, except in the far north and much of the Mediterranean fringes. They enter gardens in places, but do not settle down like park deer can be seen to do.

HABITS

Roe lead solitary lives, except during the rut, and have characteristic barks, but you may see small groups in winter. The annual growth of the antlers takes place in the winter, rather than summer, months. Twin fawns are usual, and the July rut follows a few weeks after their birth. There is a smaller rut in September. Adults are dark grey/brown in winter, with two pale throat patches, but go bright foxy-red in summer. Roe deer will stamp and froth at the mouth when angry.

The long, mobile ears of roe deer look even larger on the does. Both sexes have white patches on black muzzles. If a doe feels that her young are in danger, she will attack with her sharp hooves.

ROE DEER
L 90–135cm. Fawns are spotted. They follow the doe after a few days, hiding in one place between feeds.

MUNTJAC
L 80–90cm. Introduced from China to S England. Smallest wild deer in Europe. One fawn born about every seven months. The doe will mate soon after the young are born. Dark in winter, light brown in summer. They bark, and scent-mark scrapes on frayed trees. When disturbed, may click teeth and show white underside of tail. Buck is in velvet in the summer.

The Chinese water deer ▷ (L 75–100cm) has been introduced to S England from China, and is the only species in Europe without antlers. Note the long canines used in conflicts instead of antlers. Muntjac (middle) have long pedicles with little antlers that develop single, upward pointing tines. Roe (right) develop three-tined antlers with sharp uneven bone at the base.

CHINESE WATER DEER   **MUNTJAC**   **ROE**

TRACKER POINTS

Frayed tree

Mud print

Bucks wear off their velvet on young trees and branches. They scent-mark these, too, and thrash them, in preparation for encounters with rivals. Roe and Chinese water deer prints are similar about 4.5cm long, but muntjac are smaller, about 3cm. Roes may court round bushes to make a ring in the rut.

Roe ring

FALLOW DEER

FALLOW DEER
L 130–150cm. A mature buck jumps well, and can get under fences. The neck thickens prior to the rut, and he becomes exhausted by so much fighting, mating and calling.

HABITATS

Fallow deer are most easily seen in parks, but woodland is their natural home. They are very variable in colour, from black to white, but the usual summer coat is spotted brown. In winter, most become a drab dark brown or black.

HABITS

Fallows rut around October and November when the bucks make loud groaning calls to defend a territory. Antlers clash as rival bucks fight to round up does, and you can scent their strong odours, especially in scrapes and the soil around these sites. Single fawns are born seven months later. The bucks lie up in cover during the summer as their new antlers develop.

Fawns are born in mid June and have a speckled coat to hide them amongst foliage. They are left between feeds by their mother until strong enough to walk with her.

◀ **SIKA DEER**
▼ **AXIS DEER**
L 100–155cm and 130cm respectively. Two spotted deer introduced locally in Europe, which stay spotted all year long. Both have a single fawn in summer.

TRACKER POINTS

Hooves print well in soft mud, and can help tell which deer are present. Droppings vary from dry winter pellets to often sticky ones in the summer. Cast antlers may be gnawed by rodents or may be chewed by the deer themselves.

Deer, such as fallow, cast ▲ their antlers and re-grow them in 'velvet' skin annually. This is cleaned off and bone left.

NORTHERN DEER

REINDEER
L 130–270cm. Reindeer
undertake long seasonal
migrations and, like all deer,
can run fast to evade
predators when necessary.

HABITATS

Deer in the remote habitats of N Europe have
to withstand harsh winter conditions, limited
variety of vegetation and hot summers with
flies to both them. Reindeer, elk and the white-
tailed deer, introduced from N America to
Finland, are found in Scandinavia eastwards.

HABITS

Reindeer are kept in domestic herds in many
parts of Scandinavia, but this ancient farming
method has been affected by radiation damage
to the tundra, lichens and other plants. Wild
populations also survive. Calves, born early
summer, are quickly able to join the herd.
Calves are unspotted, and are born in summer.

The vast bull elk has wide,
flat antlers with points
(palmate) which are more
spiky in European race. It has
a long pendulum of hair on
throat. Likes to feed wading
in water.

Note how the white-tailed 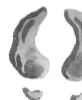 buck's antlers turn forward over the head, and the tail flares white underneath.

Elk have rather horse-like ▷ noses which droop over their mouths, and the males call with a bugle noise in the rut. When two males in a rut come into contact with one another, they will fight quite violently.

Reindeer have large feet to cope with snow, and the rounded hooves click as they walk to keep the herd in touch in blizzards.

PROJECT

Deer can be attracted by special calls available in some sports shops, or you might find a plastic toy gives a very high squeak. Keep hidden, downwind. Do not pipe away like an alarm clock, but be patient and give gaps between calls. Try elsewhere if nothing happens after 15 minutes. You may be barked at in response and a female deer may run up, anxious in case her fawn is making the noise. Once you have seen her, retire quietly.

RED DEER

The hind lacks antlers, but ▷ deer can be very protective using hooves and teeth.

RED DEER
L 120–260cm. Foxy red coat in summer; grey/brown coat in winter.

HABITATS

Red deer are found across Europe in woodland, moors and grassland, even in desert scrub. In Britain the largest numbers are on moors and upland grass areas in the Highlands, but populations survive in north-west England and some southern woodland areas.

HABITS

A really exciting wild animal to watch during the autumn rut, when the stags drive off rivals with roaring challenges, clashes of antlers and dramatic fights to secure a 'harem' of hinds. Frosty weather in late September is a good time to visit the traditional rutting areas, and you may find muddy wallows where the stags have rolled to enhance their body scent.

Antlers usually number five to six tines on each side, getting larger until the stag is in its teens in the wild – this specimen has 42 tines!

Red deer are more easily observed in parks or woods. Because they are used to people walking past in parks, you may find that they remain still while being observed, and allow you a good opportunity for closer observation and an attractive photograph.

HOW TO FIND

Ask forestry rangers and wardens for good stalking areas, and always approach likely areas downwind. In exposed mountain or moorland areas you will have to crawl and use available cover to approach for good viewing with your binoculars. Look out for wary deer on the edge of the herd – even in a park – which alert the others: all can vanish away into cover if an intruder is detected.

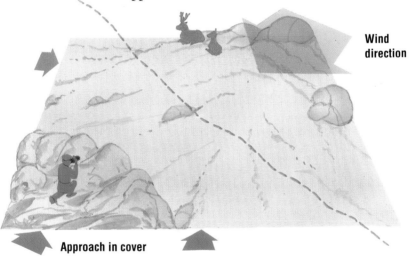

Wind direction

Approach in cover

TRACKER POINTS

Because red deer like to wallow in swampy ground, you will easily spot the tracks that they make (left). The sound of clashing antlers or thrashing of trees, and loud bellowing roars, is a sign that you should not approach mating stags.

WHALES

The high fin is distinctive in killer whales. They usually swim in small pods (groups). Very sharp teeth. ▷

KILLER WHALE
L 9m. Killer whales hunt whales and seals as well as large fish. Can knock seals off ice sheets, or surprise them at beaches.

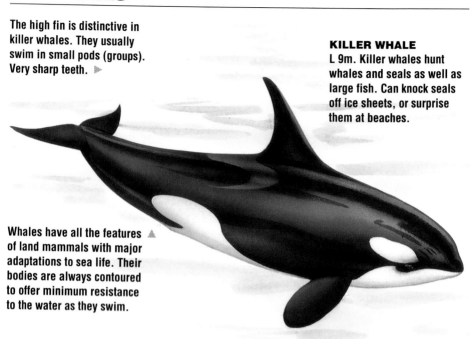

Whales have all the features ▲ of land mammals with major adaptations to sea life. Their bodies are always contoured to offer minimum resistance to the water as they swim.

HABITATS

All whales (cetaceans) live entirely in the sea, unlike seals which return to breed and moult on shore. They breath through blowholes on the top of their heads. Some of the larger species are seen in Europe as they pass by during migration. Due to hunting, pollution and drift net fishing, all species are becoming less common.

HABITS

Slow to breed, and with a long lifespan, they have one young at a time after about 12 months' gestation period. The young are born and suckled in the water, and most species move about in schools or groups. Some lack teeth, and strain water through tough horned plates fringed with bristles (called baleen) that trap the plankton on which they feed. Most species, however, have teeth.

You may see killer whales or other cetaceans from the land, on the edge of fiords or lochs. Sharks usually reveal a second tail fin which is vertical. Dolphin tail flukes are always horizontal.

BEAKED WHALES ▽

Beaked whales, such as Cuvier's (L 8m), Sowerby's (L 5m) and the Bottlenose (L 8m), are little studied and only rarely seen. They possess just one pair of sharp teeth like little tusks in the lower jaw, and dive deep for squid and cuttlefish.

CUVIER'S

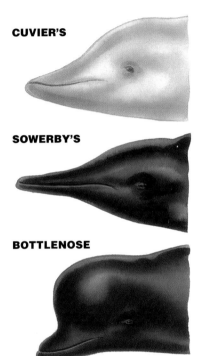

SOWERBY'S

BOTTLENOSE

Whales break free of the water for various ▲ reasons, including communication with others, fish disturbance and simply in play. They look for distant signs of food, such as feeding gulls, and may stay head up, vertically in the water to view the surroundings. Look for the contrasting patterns on a killer whale as it leaps high out of the water – many marine observers are able to identify individual killer whales from their markings.

Strandings are a tragic ▲ sight on beaches. Groups of pilot whales are the most often found. Earth magnetic fields, or pursuit of food, are suspected reasons.

GREAT WHALES

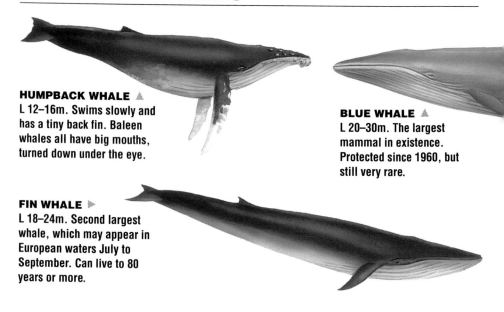

HUMPBACK WHALE ▲
L 12–16m. Swims slowly and has a tiny back fin. Baleen whales all have big mouths, turned down under the eye.

BLUE WHALE ▲
L 20–30m. The largest mammal in existence. Protected since 1960, but still very rare.

FIN WHALE ▷
L 18–24m. Second largest whale, which may appear in European waters July to September. Can live to 80 years or more.

HABITATS

The rarity of the great whales around Europe is due to centuries of hunting. Even protection has only seen a very slow recovery in some species. Migration takes the baleen whales into the cold northern waters to feed on krill, which are tiny crustaceans eaten in vast quantities in the summer. They move south in winter to have their young in the warm water of the southern oceans.

Humpback

HABITS

Humpback whales call with dramatic sounds underwater, and can breach clear of the water's surface. Their very long fins are distinctive, and individuals can be recognised by the pattern of markings on the tail flukes. Even the way the larger whales breath can help in identification. When they surface they 'blow' a characteristic spout. In the case of the sperm whale this is at a unique oblique angle.

Sperm

Whilst the humpback has a distinctive curved fin, the sperm whale has not much more than a triangular bump to show.

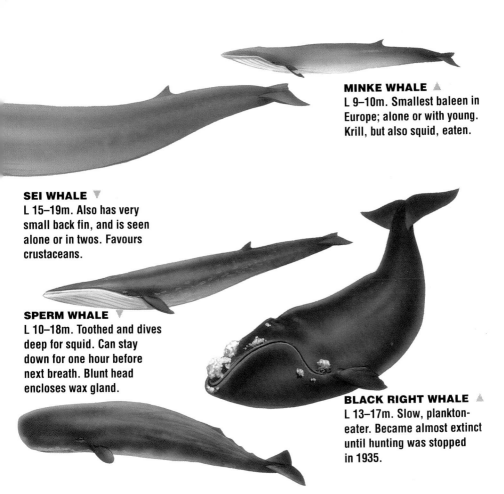

MINKE WHALE ▲
L 9–10m. Smallest baleen in Europe; alone or with young. Krill, but also squid, eaten.

SEI WHALE ▽
L 15–19m. Also has very small back fin, and is seen alone or in twos. Favours crustaceans.

SPERM WHALE ▽
L 10–18m. Toothed and dives deep for squid. Can stay down for one hour before next breath. Blunt head encloses wax gland.

BLACK RIGHT WHALE ▲
L 13–17m. Slow, plankton-eater. Became almost extinct until hunting was stopped in 1935.

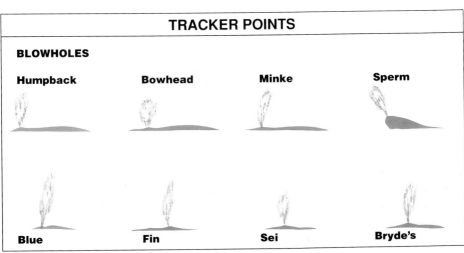

TRACKER POINTS

BLOWHOLES

Humpback   Bowhead   Minke   Sperm

Blue   Fin   Sei   Bryde's

DOLPHINS AND PORPOISES

HABITATS

There are few more exciting sights in mammal-watching than seeing the great whales, dolphins and porpoises at sea. You may see them by chance from ferries on holiday, or be surprised as you quietly watch for other species on the edge of remote lakes open to the sea.

HABITS

Their movements relate to food and breeding. The great whales commute between Polar and tropical seas, and smaller species follow shoals of fish to coastal waters.

Dolphin schools
Common dolphin schools are the most frequently seen species in the Mediterranean and English Channel. Note 'hour-glass' shape on sides, usually with yellow to front. May leap out of the water together as they swim, as if in a synchronized swimming team. Associated with shipping. The fin is more pointed than in porpoise (below right).

◀ **BOTTLE-NOSED DOLPHIN**
L 2–4m. Large, grey and playful. Often shown in dolphinaria. One young per 12–month pregnancy.

◀ **RISSO'S DOLPHIN**
L 3–4m. No beak. Feeds on squid and cuttlefish, hence scars received during sea-floor foraging.

Boat trips to watch whales
are more and more popular.
You need good binoculars,
and may have only a brief
time to spot the features
which identify each species
as they breach the water, or
play amongst the wake of
larger vessels passing by.
These beluga whales were
photographed feeding in the
Arctic Sea.

COMMON DOLPHIN
L 1–2m. Obvious patterns
and a narrow beak. The fin
curves backwards.

WHITE-SIDED DOLPHIN
L 2–3m. High fin, with black
head and back. Large; more
in N Europe. Lacks the long
beak of most dolphins.

PORPOISE
L 1.5–2m. Does not leap like
dolphins. Slow swimmer
around coasts and estuaries.
No beak.

INDEX

ILLUSTRATIONS BY

Priscilla Barrett 30–31, 48–51, 72–75 · Bernard Thornton Artists: Jim Channell 7, 20–21, 40–41, 60–61, 118–125; Robert Morton 112–117 · Sarah Castell 6, 8 · David Lewis: Robert Cook 4, 24–25 · The Gallery: Angela Hargreaves 26–29 · Garden Studios: David Ashby 8, 12–13; Graham Austin 70–71; Shirley Felts cover; David Holmes 94–95; Doreen McGuinness 22–23, 32–39, 42–47, 52–59, 62–69, 76–89, 92–93, 100–111 · Ian Fleming Associates: John Butler 90–91 · Maltings Partnership 9–11, 14–19 · Linden Artists: Phil Weare 98–99 · 2-D: Roy Wiltshire 5, 96–97.

The publishers would like to thank the following organisations and individuals for their kind permission to reproduce the photographs in this book:

Sarah Castell 6 above, 49, 75 · Michael Clark 5 below, 11 below, 17 below, 19 below, 20, 23, 27, 33, 45, 53, 59, 65, 86, 89 below, 90, 91, 99, 112, 117, 118 · Eric and David Hosking 111; · D.P. Wilson 29 · Nature Photographers: Front cover, 25; S.C. Bisserot 55, 57, 95; Kevin Carlson 67 top, 89 above; Colin Carver 98; Jean Hall 109; E.A. Janes 21, 31; Hugh Miles 60, 101, 125; C.K. Mylne 26; O. Newman 19 above, 37, 73; W. Paton 119; Paul Sterry 6 centre, 39, 50, 81, 83, 120; Roger Tidman 61 top left, 85, 105, 107 · NHPA: G.I. Bernard 9 above, 19 centre; E.A. Janes 93; Walter Murray 61 top right; Jany Sauvanet 103 · Octopus Group Picture Library 35.